CXC English

Peter Roberts

Department of Language and Linguistics
University of the West Indies, Barbados

CAMBRIDGE
UNIVERSITY PRESS

CAMBRIDGE UNIVERSITY PRESS
Cambridge, New York, Melbourne, Madrid, Cape Town, Singapore, São Paulo, Delhi

Cambridge University Press
The Water Club, Beach Road, Granger Bay, Cape Town 8005, South Africa

www.cambridge.org
Information on this title: www.cambridge.org/9780521429023

First published 1994
5th printing 2008

Printed in the United Kingdom at the University Press, Cambridge

ISBN 978-0-521-42902-3 paperback
. . . .

Cover photograph by Tony Stone Worldwide
Cover designed by Chris McLeod

Contents

To the Teacher

Theory and philosophy behind the text

The Caribbean Examinations Council states that its syllabus is based on the following:

The need to use language skills and insights to

(i) acquire and communicate factual information

(ii) discriminate between and evaluate views and opinions expressed by others

(iii) express personal views rationally and persuasively

(iv) communicate personal experience and insights, and

(v) enjoy and derive satisfaction from language used in its various art forms to communicate penetrative insights into human experience.

Language skills and insights are tested under two broad headings by CXC – **Understanding** and **Expression**. At the Basic Level 60% is given for questions which test Understanding and 40% for questions which test Expression. At the General Level 44% is given for Understanding and 56% for Expression.

This book has the same general objectives as the CXC syllabus. It realises, as does CXC, that detailed syllabuses often have a 'tyrannical influence on what pupils are exposed to in the classroom' no matter how wholesome and healthy the general objectives are. This textbook is intended for pupils in the final year of preparation of the CXC syllabus; it selects certain topics which can be better handled in the final year and explores them in a penetrative way. After having gone through all the units, pupils will be ready for the CXC examination.

This textbook was developed on the theory that in the final year of the syllabus, emphasis must be placed on **Expression**, because productive skills are based on and are more difficult than receptive skills. In any case, improving productive language skills will also improve receptive language skills. The more a pupil *writes*, the more his or her comprehension of the words, sentences and idioms of the English language will improve. Although this book does not contain exercises specifically called 'comprehension', **Understanding** is an integral part of each unit, so that pupils' comprehension skills will improve as they work their way through the book.

Writing requires skills which are active and creative. Reading widely is helpful and should be encouraged, but reading by itself does not require concentration on all of the details of spelling, punctuation, word choice and sentence structure. Such concentration comes only from having to write constantly. Knowledge of a language is like an iceberg – there is much more below the surface (receptive skills) than above it (productive skills). What this means is that only a minor part of what pupils are taught and what pupils learn will show up in pupils' actual performance. Teaching and learning therefore have to go over and beyond what pupils are expected to produce consistently. As a teacher you should always remember the iceberg.

This text was developed specifically for Caribbean pupils and, in keeping with the CXC philosophy, pursues a holistic approach to language. Accordingly, it should not be used in patchwork manner with the intention of curing problem areas. Many of the exercises set require that pupils become accustomed to reading longer passages and writing longer answers. The theory behind this is that:

(i) there is no other way to learn to write than by writing

(ii) it is only by writing paragraphs and essays that pupils will learn to write sentences.

Structure of the text

a) Topics of the individual units

There are 24 units in this book, each unit representing roughly a week's work through the final year.

The opening unit – on essay writing – serves as the foundation unit for the book as a whole, reflecting the emphasis placed on Expression in the final year of the CXC syllabus.

The units in the first half of the book (Units 2–13) relate to CXC stated need (v) and are concerned primarily with artistic writing – with the focus on the short story and the poem. Teachers should find the units on poetry particularly useful in teaching an area for which a great deal of guidance is not usually given and which many pupils shy away from.

Units 14–22 are concerned with factual writing: personal and formal letters [relating to CXC stated need (iv)]; the language of argument and advertising [CXC stated needs (ii) and (iii)]; understanding and giving information [CXC stated need (i)]. In all these units, pupils are encouraged to consider how language changes according to user, context and purpose.

The closing units (Units 23 and 24) look at spoken language, specifically the difficulties which pupils may encounter in moving from spoken to written language. The influence of dialect and non-standard English as it is spoken throughout the Caribbean is a recurring theme of the book. Units 23 and 24 deal explicitly with important differences between non-standard oral English and standard written English, as well as differences between speech and writing in Standard English.

b) Topics across units

Selection of material across units is also possible. For example, if a teacher wants to concentrate on essay writing specifically, the following sections can be used in addition to the guidance and exercises given in Unit 1:

      Unit 2 – Guidance: Planning a story

      Unit 16 – Guidance: What is an argument?
            Language: The language of argument

      Unit 19 – Guidance: Expository writing

      Unit 20 – Guidance: Organising information
            Language: Writing clearly
            Sentence composition: Verb style and noun style

Another topic which occurs across units is the difference between surface meaning and deeper meanings and ambiguity. The teacher can follow this topic across the units by using the following sections:

      Unit 8 – Guidance: Different tones of voice
            Sentence composition: Ambiguous sentences

      Unit 11 – Guidance: Double meaning; figurative language;
            allusions

      Unit 14 – Language: Sentence composition: Auxiliary verbs

c) Structure of each unit

Each unit opens with a list of objectives setting out what the unit intends to achieve so that the teacher can direct the pupils' attention accordingly.

    The unit is then sub-divided into two main sections – Section A: Guidance; and Section B: Language work.

Section A: Guidance gives useful information and advice to both teacher and pupils, and uses a wide range of stimulus material to illustrate and contextualise the guidance given. The stimulus material includes: extracts from novels and short stories, poems, factual writing (newspaper articles, advertisements, reports of science experiments, etc.). Most of the writing comes from the Caribbean.

A wide range of assignments provides pupils with the opportunity to practise what they have learned, mostly through extended pieces of writing, but also through class and group discussion, dramatisation, etc.

The teacher may use this section according to the needs of the class and of individual pupils. He or she may choose to work systematically through it with the pupils, or to focus on the stimulus material, using the notes as background information to class discussion. The teacher also has to determine whether some sections (e.g. writing up of science experiments) are relevant to all pupils.

Section B: Language work includes the following sub-sections: Language; Sentence composition; Vocabulary; Spelling; Punctuation. These do not all feature in every unit.

Various types of exercises are included throughout each unit – questions on stimulus material, multiple choice, completion of words and sentences, filling in blanks, error detection, etc. By doing a variety of exercises pupils become familiar with all the possibilities that might arise in an examination. Some exercises are designed to encourage pupils to produce words and structures which many of them do not use in their everyday speech, for example, the use of adjectives and adjective phrases in describing people and things; the correct use of 'have' and 'had' as auxiliaries.

The context of exercises is not always restricted to the guidance or points which immediately precede the exercises. The exercises are meant to integrate pupils' previous experience with current guidance. In such cases, some pupils may need additional guidance from the teacher.

Writing an Essay

Objectives

This unit will help you to:

✓ understand what an essay is
✓ plan an essay
✓ develop ideas in paragraphs
✓ see how essays can be used to express opinions
✓ be able to compare and contrast when writing essays
✓ know what a sentence is

Section A
Guidance

What is an essay?

An essay is a short composition in which a writer analyses a topic or voices his/her opinion on a subject. Essays are a common form of exercise at school, but they also are a normal part of newspapers (e.g. news reports, letters to the editor) and magazines.

Four steps to follow in essay writing:

1 Decide what you are going to do

2 Make a plan

3 Write

4 Re-read and correct

1 Decide what you are going to do

- Be sure that you understand what each topic set requires, before you make your choice.

- Select a topic that you find interesting and that you know about.

- Work out or find out how much time you have for the essay. You should know from previous experience how much time you need to spend on planning, writing and re-reading. You may find that you need to spend only three quarters of the time on actual writing.

2 Make a plan

- Think of and write down ideas, points and other information as they occur to you. (If you have difficulty doing this, look at page 21 in Unit 2, which deals with systems you can use to think up ideas.)

- Prepare an essay plan: work out your beginning, body and conclusion; identify the topic of each paragraph and the sub-topics to be dealt with in each paragraph.

- Decide on an interesting or effective start to your essay.

3 Write

- Use the essay plan that you have written to write the essay.
- Write as quickly but as thoughtfully as you can.

4 Re-read and correct

- Check each of the following by re-reading at least twice, once for sense and once for correctness:

the sense of what you have written

the structure of each sentence

the punctuation of each sentence

the spelling of the words

Planning an essay

Read the following essay written by a student.

Causes of auto-mobile accidents

As the number of fatal accidents and other incidents on the road increases, people are of the belief that it is never their fault. Whose fault is it then? The road's, the street light's? Of course not. It is the fault of us imperfect humans who choose to drive negligently. Accidents also occur as a result of a faulty car, or when building equipment and other obstacles are in the road, or from driving when intoxicated.

Negligence is a major problem that the police must deal with because other people do not seem to care. They seem to believe that the rules are only there to prevent them from having fun. I jump out of my skin when I see people go through red lights, not thinking that they may come upon an unknowing pedestrian crossing the street. Others drive 'by guess and by God', not paying attention to the road and going at unbelievable speeds. I doubt anyone could guess from them what the speed limit is. Street regulations have become somewhat of a joke. Hand signals are another case, people doing all kinds of gesticulating that would have anyone confused. When they are going to stop, people should stop somewhere where they would not put themselves in danger, but that is not the case. They stop anywhere for a chat or other unjustifiable reasons, not thinking that they could be hit from here to Helsinki.

The problems mentioned are blamed on the younger folk, but at least they care about the upkeep of their cars. There are some cars, rather pieces of metal, that look as if they would fall apart if they went into a deep pothole. These vehicles have lights missing, brakes that work when they want to and engines that cause noise and air pollution.

The pieces of boxes, trees, building materials and litter in the road also pose a problem. They cause traffic to come to a standstill. As a result, people become anxious and angry and look for the easiest and quickest way to pass these obstacles. These people often find their way into a collision. There are also those pedestrians and bicyclists who seem to own the road. Therefore cars behind them have to anticipate their motion, making it difficult for the vehicles to overtake them.

Another way people try to kill themselves is by driving under the influence of alcohol and/or illegal drugs. What possesses these persons I do not know. They must have the distinct urge to commit suicide or murder. People have fun and drive without a care in the world, not realising that the party is over when they get on the road.

Like all other accidents, automobile accidents do not happen by chance, but by chances people take with their judgement, their health and their vehicles.

Exercises

1   Identify the introduction, the body and the conclusion of the essay.

2   What is the topic in each paragraph?

3   Are the ideas logically presented? Give reasons for your answer.

Parts of an essay

Introduction

Paragraph 1
Either: state your view and prepare the reader for what is going to come
Or: tell the reader what you are going to discuss in the body of the essay.

Body

Paragraph 2
Make a point and develop it.

Paragraph 3
Make another point and develop it.

Paragraph 4
Make another point and develop it.

Conclusion

Paragraph 5
Either: bring together your points
Or: make an overall judgement of them.
Leave the reader with a clear view of what you are saying.

Here are two examples of an essay plan.

---

1 The computer

INTRODUCTION

Para 1:   I will say what it is
I will show its advantages
I will show its disadvantages
I will come to a conclusion

BODY

Para 2:   Parts of a computer
Artificial intelligence

Para 3:   Why people like it
It saves time by doing tasks quickly
It stores information which can be retrieved at
the touch of a button
It organises information in various ways

Para 4:   Why people fear it
Inability to use it
Belief that it requires unusual skill
Belief that it will replace workers

CONCLUSION

Para 5:   I will compare its advantages with its
disadvantages and say whether the former
outweigh the latter.

---

2 **Juvenile delinquency**

INTRODUCTION

Definition   A problem of every generation
                    Unacceptable behaviour by young people

BODY

Causes

Home life: idleness and lack of supervision,
                    broken homes

School life: lack of guidance/counselling
                    truants, drop-outs, under-achievers

Effects

Minor offences: traffic violations, vandalism
Major offences: assaults, burglaries, drug dealing

CONCLUSION

Remedies

Recreation: competitive sports for young people,
                 involvement in club activities
Work: agencies to place young people in jobs

Exercise   Write an essay plan for each of the following topics:

1   Christmas or any religious festival

2   Illegal drugs

3   Pop music or Gospel music

4   Racial discrimination

5   Africa or India or China

How to develop your ideas in paragraphs

- Identify the points: in the same way that in a recipe you identify the ingredients, in an essay you also have to identify points that make up the subject matter.

- Arrange the points in proper order: in telling a story relate the events in the order in which they happened; in explaining how something is done, start with what you do first and end with what you do last; in describing, move from big subjects to small subjects or vice versa.

- Establish (where relevant) cause and effect: try to distinguish between real, deep-seated causes and apparent, immediate ones; try to distinguish between short-term effects or results and long-term ones.

- Compare and contrast: show how points are similar to and different from other relevant ones.

- Illustrate your points: use actual examples in order to make your points easier to follow; good examples are usually very forceful.

- Support arguments with statistics: facts and figures can be manipulated to win arguments; try to be honest in your use of these.

- Quote from speeches, documents or other materials: quotations give your writing style; they also give the impression that you read and listen to others.

Expressing opinions in essays

Whether people are writing essays for schoolwork or newspaper articles, they will be giving their opinion on the particular topic. It is important to be able to distinguish between what is an opinion and what is fact.

Here are two essays expressing opposing opinions about AIDS.

Alexander's essay

I strongly disagree that victims of the killer disease AIDS should be kept isolated as lepers were in previous times, as this act is not only inhumane but serves to conceal the ills and immorality present in our society now.

AIDS is a disease caused by a virus and is common among homosexuals, intravenous drug users and amongst prostitutes also. This might seem to be prevalent in only a small section of the population, but taking into account the promiscuity outside and within the boundary of marriage, it surely is not restricted.

However, to condemn these people to isolation for the remainder of their limited lives is inhumane and unacceptable, as they no doubt regret their past actions. They happen to have feelings and desires like anyone else and the mere thought of having the killer disease will, of course, terrify them.

Isolating someone is infringing on their constitutional right to live and move about freely in society. The only possible remedy or antidote is for the society to develop proper moral scruples and a change in sexual habits.

Sasha's essay

I agree totally with the statement that victims of the killer disease AIDS should be kept isolated from society, because they provide a grave threat to everyone that they become intimate with.

Most people that suffer from AIDS are very selfish and they adopt the attitude that they are not going to die alone, they are going to try and take as many friends and other people down with them as possible. The fact that they would want to inflict this dreaded disease on others makes me want to take evasive action now.

People with so-called knowledge of the AIDS virus say that it is very hard to get AIDS. That may be true only if everyone were honest enough to admit that they had the disease before any sexual relationship with any sane person. I do not think that honesty is stronger than the sex drive.

I do have sympathy for the AIDS victims, but only from afar. The only way that I can see us controlling this disease is by taking all the victims to an isolated island and letting it die out.

Exercises

1   Read through each essay and make a note of the *facts* they each give, i.e. statements with which no-one could disagree. Then from each essay give two examples of statements which express the author's personal opinion.

2   Which essay do you feel is more successful in expressing the author's opinions? Give reasons.

Assignments

A   Here are a number of first sentences for essays. Think of a suitable topic for each one and then complete the first paragraph of the essay.

1   Sooner or later the subject of money always comes up.

2   There is not now and there never has been one clear answer to the question of abortion.

3   Running a successful operation is no mystery.

4   There are two ways to go about preparing ground for planting.

5   Part of the excitement of a new school year is seeing your friends again (probably your enemies too) and talking, or boasting, about what you did during the summer holidays.

6   By the beginning of the 1950s there were signs that the old order was breaking down.

B   Attempt as many as possible of the following essay topics.

1   Write the annual report on the activities of a club.

2   Write an interesting report on a match between a team which you like and a rival team.

3   Write about a tour you went on. Try to convince those who paid for it why it should or should not be done again.

4   Imagine you were Nelson Mandela. Explain to a person in the West Indies the problems of being in prison for over twenty years.

5   Explain the principles of your religion to a person who is not a member of the religion.

6   You have to explain, by telephone, to a member of your class who is ill what you did in class today and the homework for tomorrow. Prepare beforehand and write out what you are going to tell him/her.

7   Read out to the class what is in a letter which you found under your neighbour's chair.

8   Explain and describe who was the best-looking person at a party you went to.

9   Explain the political system of your country to a person in India.

10   Show why it is important for you to preserve and express your culture in your everyday life.

11   Explain to a person in Hong Kong the different races of people in your country, how they came to be there, and how they get on with each other.

12   In response to an old person who is always boasting about 'the good old days', show how these days are much better.

13   Explain to your grandfather or an old relative what a computer is, what you think it is used for now and what you think it may be used for in the future.

14   Present a case for preserving the art of story-telling.

**Section B
Language
work**

Language: Comparing and contrasting

When writing essays one useful technique is to be able to compare and contrast. In *comparison* you are identifying things that are alike. In *contrast* you are identifying things that are different.

Here are a few pointers in the organisation of an essay dealing with comparisons and contrasts:

- Arrange points under headings: according to clear, visible and concrete features (e.g. colour, number, size, weight); and according to value (e.g. usefulness, worth, performance, achievement).

- Choose one of two methods of comparing/contrasting in an essay:

  1 One thing completely + other thing completely + synthesis
  This is a simple method in which you describe/analyse one of the things which you are dealing with completely. Then you describe the other, and, as an ending, conclude with an assessment in which you look at crucial points in the two.

  2 Point by point + summary
  This is a more difficult method in which you pick out crucial points in the two things for comparison/contrast, deal with them one by one, after which you summarise and conclude.

- Pay attention to parallelism in sentence structure. Compare/contrast like with like (= parallelism), noun with noun, verb with verb, adjective with adjective, theory with theory, people with people, argument with argument. E.g.

  Not 'Democracy is good whereas anarchists are bad.'

  but 'Democracy is good whereas anarchy is bad.'

Sentence composition

It is easy to identify sentences already written. Each one normally begins with a capital letter and ends with a full stop. In order to write good sentences in your essays, it helps if you know about how they are made up as well as the words used to describe parts of sentences.

You should already know words like:

noun   verb   adjective   adverb   pronoun   conjunction

You also need to know the words used to describe parts of a sentence, words like:

subject   predicate   object   clause   phrase

This knowledge will help you when you are re-reading your work to check that your sentences are really sentences. It will also help you to vary the type of sentences you write.

What is a sentence?

A sentence can be one word or any number of words, but every sentence, no matter how long or short it is, is made up of a *subject* and *predicate*. Of course, if you take a number of short sentences and join them with 'and', 'but', 'or', you will have more than one subject and more than one predicate.

Consider the following sentences:

	Subject	*Predicate*	
1	The cat	sat on the mat.	(The subject is a noun)
2	He	went.	(The subject is a pronoun, i.e. a word used instead of a noun)
3		Go.	(Subject 'you' is understood)
4	Seeing	is believing.	(Subject is 'seeing'; a verbal noun)
5	Jogging at night	is dangerous.	(Subject is a phrase; 'jogging at night')
6	That he knows	bothers me.	(Subject is a clause; 'that he knows')

A *clause* is a part inside a sentence which itself contains a subject and predicate.

Exercise

In whatever books you have available look for examples of sentences similar to those given above. Make a note of them and bring them to class. Make a note also of any sentences where you cannot decide which is the subject and which is the predicate.

Analysing a Story

Objectives

This unit will help you to:

✓ plan and create a story using systems
✓ analyse stories
✓ distinguish between main and subordinate verbs
✓ understand the main reasons for punctuation

Section A Guidance

Story-telling forms a part of the heritage of the West Indies. Story-telling on moonlit nights was common throughout the West Indies before electricity, radio and television became normal. The best-known short stories are Anancy or Nancy stories. Even today Nancy stories and Brer Rabbit stories are popular among children in some islands.

Planning a story

Although telling a story and writing a story involve different skills, the 'story' remains the same. Often the biggest difficulties which you may have in writing a story are that after you have written the first few lines you don't know what to say next, you run out of material or you have told the whole story in only a couple of lines. These problems can be cured in all cases by planning, which involves using a system. There are three simple systems which you can use to help create material and spread the material out in a reasonable way.

Using a system to create a story

These systems are guides only and should not be followed slavishly every time you write. In fact, you should first try to write freely (let your mind wander on its own, write down whatever occurs to you). Then expand and improve your components, your language, your ideas by using any or all of the three systems.

First system: Using question words

The simplest system which makes sure that you cover all areas one by one is by using the words

who   what   where   why   when   how

Take, for example, the familiar topic 'A day at the beach':

who   Who went with me?
Who was at the beach?
Who was not at the beach?

what   What did I/we take?
What is normally at the beach?
What was at the beach that day?

where   Which beach, where in the country?
Which part of the beach?

why   Why did we go to the beach – to play, swim, exercise?
Did we have to?

when   What time of the day?
What time of the year?

how   How did we get there?
How long did we stay?
How was the weather?

By this simple system you can build up an essay or story of any length.

Second system: The five senses

Another system which you can use to make sure that your descriptions are detailed and interesting is to relate each of the five senses in turn to your topic. The five senses are:

sight touch taste smell hearing

Sight   – relates to colours (blue, green, etc.) shapes (geometrical, natural) sizes.

Touch   – relates to texture (rough, smooth) feel (hot, wet).

Taste   – whereas taste relates in most cases to food and drink, it can refer to things which literally (by inhaling) or metaphorically 'leave a taste in your mouth'.

Smell   – you should try not only to give your reactions to smell (i.e. pleasant/unpleasant), but also to identify or describe the smell accurately.

Hearing – this relates, of course, both to human voices (therefore to language, conversations, etc.) and to other sounds (animals, machines, falling objects, etc.).

Third system: Areas of behaviour

Another system, which requires an understanding of certain terms, relates to areas of human behaviour. The list in this case is not set, as in the first and second systems, but can be added to. Here are some areas:

> *religious, political, economic, social, psychological, sexual, moral, legal, artistic, historical.*

Of course, not all will be relevant to your topic. You can relate these concepts to the essay topic illustrated in the First system above in the following way:

Religious

My friend was not at the beach that day because it was his Sabbath.

A religious group was at the beach and its leader was baptising new converts.

Political/social

We were bathing at a beach that was rocky because the Government had allowed hotels and rich people to buy the best beaches.

Sexual

The boys whistled at the girls when they passed by in bikinis.

Couples came to the beach to court and not to bathe.

Exercises

1   Use the First system to write out a list of ideas for the topic 'My grandmother'. (You do not have to stick to one of your real grandmothers. You may, if you wish, make up things. However, always keep a specific person in mind.)

2   Use the Second system to write out a list of ideas for a topic dealing with the inside of a church, mosque or temple during a religious service.

3   Use the Third system to write out a list of ideas for the topic 'Abuse of young people by adults'.

4   Use parts of all three systems to make a list of ideas for the topic 'Parents of today'.

Using a system to analyse stories

In the same way that you can use these three systems to create material for your story, you can use them to dissect any story or essay that has already been written. Each system can be used to cover a different area of analysis.

The First system covers the components/plot/context of the story.

The Second system deals with the language and style.

The Third system focuses on themes or ideas occurring in the story/essay.

Read this simple story.

Man struck with gru gru stick

As a boy I had often been asked whether I was afraid of spirits or jumbies. My answer had always been: 'I don't know. I have never seen any'. Little did I suspect how soon I would be subjected to a very severe test.

My father worked at the Colony Hospital and, as a young fellow, I often went up there to sleep with him. I usually left very early in the morning for home, in time for school.

One very dark morning, about five o'clock, I was returning home along the road which is thickly studded with huge mahogany trees, when I had the scare of my life. When going along this road at night or before daybreak, one gets the impression that one is travelling through a dark tunnel. Well, as I was approaching the crossroads, I seemed to discern in the distance a dark object approaching me on the same side of the road on which I was walking. I therefore thought that I would go to the opposite or left side. On doing this, however, I experienced a slight bit of fear when I observed that the object also shifted back to my side and was apparently heading straight for me. Nearer and nearer we came. Higher and higher mounted my fears. It now seemed to me that a collision was imminent. I could not understand the reason for this. At last after a few more steps, we came within arm's length, by which time my fear had reached its peak. I then raised my gru gru stick and brought it down with all the force I could muster. Then I felt my stick grasped and I heard: 'Hold, hold, hold, it's me, Springer'. I was so annoyed that I was just able to utter a grunt of disapproval and disgust at this old man's actions, and I continued on my way home.

The next day, Springer, an old tailor, who was often called 'Big Rat' and 'Loupgarou' by the wicked boys, related the incident to my father, telling him what a brave boy I was. I know nothing about being brave. What I do know is that I was terribly frightened and therefore instinctively struck out with the only weapon that I had – my gru gru stick. I am, however, certain that if it had been a revolver instead of a stick, Springer would have been a dead man. For in my awful fright I would have shot him just as easily as I had struck him with the stick. In that case I would have been held for murder and perhaps no one would have believed my story that this man was stupidly trying to frighten me.

F.M. Coard

Exercises

1   Who? List all the people mentioned in the story and say who are the main ones.

2   What? List all the objects mentioned in the story.

3   Where? List all the places mentioned in the story.

4   Why? Why was the author on the road at that time? Why was the author annoyed?

5   When? At what time of the day/At what time of the author's life did the incident take place?

Now use the Second and Third systems to ask and answer questions about the story.

Assignments

A   One out of every five pupils should tell a story.

The pupil will have a maximum of eight minutes in which to tell the story.

Base the story on a television or radio show or on a character or incident in a book, magazine or newspaper. You may also tell a Brer Rabbit or Anancy story.

Develop your story around one main incident.

Those pupils who are not telling a story must judge each of the story-tellers, i.e. you should note down why the story was good/bad; what made the story lively; whether the story was realistic; and whatever other features of the stories you noticed. Say which story was best, second, third, etc.

B   Cut out from a recent newspaper items which you think are good material for short stories, e.g. items about fires, road accidents, crimes, sports, entertainment. Choose local events or events with which you are familiar, so that you describe in more detail the colours, buildings, people (including strange characters and personalities), vehicles, roads, trees and weather.

<table>
<tr><td>

**Section B
Language
work**

</td><td>

Sentence composition

The main verb and subordinate verb

If you came across sentences in the exercise at the end of Unit 1 which you found difficult to break up into subject and predicate, the reason might be that you were not able to spot the main verb. In a sentence of any length the main verb can be short (e.g. 'is') or long ('should have been overwhelmed').

'Main' verb implies that there may be 'subordinate' verbs. To understand the relationship between main and subordinate, consider the following sentence:

</td></tr>
</table>

> This is the cat that ate the rat that bit the man that owned the cat that ate the rat ...

A subordinate verb usually occurs with 'who', 'which', 'when', 'whom', 'where', 'how', 'that' (expressed or understood) before it. E.g.

> The man whom I knew came.

> The man I knew came.

> The man that I knew came.

'Knew' is the subordinate verb and 'came' the main verb in each case.

A subordinate verb often also occurs in a clause of its own which starts with words such as 'although', 'since', 'if', 'after'. E.g.

> Although he knew, he still came.

> He would come, if he knew.

> He came, after he knew.

> Since he came, he knew.

Exercise

Find the main verb in these five sentences and double underline it in each one. Underline all other verbs.

1   While we were waiting, he was talking on the phone as if we were intruders who had no right to be there.

2   Telling us he would be back soon, he went into the office, which was out of sight, to make a call.

3   As soon as he'd left the room, I looked at the marksheet on the desk, hoping I would see whether I had passed or not.

4   Since most of them had umbrellas, the spectators did not get soaked.

5   Although I didn't recognise him at the time, I remembered later that I had met him last year at a fete and telephoned him to apologise because I didn't want him to think that I was unfriendly.

Punctuation

Punctuation developed as a means of indicating intonation (raising and lowering of the voice, pauses, etc.) in actual speech. However, just as writing is not speech written down, punctuation is not intonation written down. The rules of punctuation have to be learnt and not guessed at from intonation.

The main uses of punctuation are:

*   to separate: the comma, semi-colon, the question mark, the full stop, the exclamation mark

*   to show that something is omitted: the apostrophe, one dot, three dots, four dots

*   to enclose: two dashes, two brackets, two commas, two sets of inverted commas

*   to link/introduce: the colon, the dash, the hyphen (See Unit 8)

Separation

Full stop (.)

The full stop separates one sentence from another.

Each full stop creates a separate sentence.

Remember to use a full stop (not a question mark) after a reported question, that is after 'ask whether ...', 'wonder if ...'. E.g.

> He asked whether I was going.
> I wonder if he is going.

Question mark (?)

This also separates one sentence from another. Remember not to use the question mark after reported/indirect questions (see above). Remember that when a sentence starts as a question, no matter how long it is, it must have a question mark at the end. It is quite easy to forget the question mark in such cases.

Exclamation mark (!)

This not only separates sentences but also marks off words uttered as exclamations.

The exclamation mark can be used for true exclamations. E.g.

Oh!

How terrible!

Help!

What a waste!

or to indicate that the words have an important rise in intonation at the end, especially when representing direct speech. E.g.

And you said you knew!

The exclamation mark should not be used when you are describing something merely to suggest emphasis.

Comma (,)

This is used in various ways:

- To separate parts of a sentence and lists in a sentence. E.g.

   For example, in their assessment of writing, females wrote significantly better than males at Grades 4, 8, and 11, the three grade levels assessed.

- To introduce or interrupt a quotation. E.g.

   'My mother is sleeping,' said the child.

- To separate elements of time. E.g.

   Saturday, 3rd June, 1915

Semi-colon (;)

This is used to separate two clauses in a sentence, sometimes where the meaning of the first contrasts in some way with that of the second. E.g.

   Pre-school children use language as a tool to communicate; they give no thought to the tool itself.

Sometimes the semi-colon is like a strong comma or a weak full stop, that is, halfway between the two. This is so in cases where parts of the sentence are already separated by commas, but where you do not want to make two separate sentences. E.g.

> Equally important, speaking and writing involve expression of oneself; therefore, differences between children's home language and that of the school may have indirect effects on writing by influencing children's self-concepts.

Note that if the author had put a comma where the semi-colon is, it would be difficult at first to follow the structure of the sentence.

Exercise

Write out this passage, restoring all the punctuation marks and capital letters.

dear mister oswald when i got to work i saw that the hurricane had blown some of the clay tiles off the top of the building so i rigged up a pulley at the top of the building and began to hoist up clay tiles in a box after i fixed the top i realised that i had hoisted up too many tiles i decided to pull the box back up and tie the rope at the bottom i then went up and filled the box with as many tiles as possible then i went down to the bottom and undid the rope unfortunately the box of tiles was heavier than i was so before i knew what was happening the box plunged down jerking me off the ground i decided to hang on and halfway up i met the box coming down it gave me a severe blow on the shoulder but i held on when i reached the top i hit my head against a beam and my fingers got squeezed in the pulley at the other end when the box hit the ground it burst into pieces which meant that there was no longer any weight at that end i therefore fell back to the ground landing on the tiles and getting severe cuts from the sharp edges at this point i must have lost consciousness because when i woke up i found myself in the hospital i respectfully request a few days sick leave yours sincerely eugene otto

Structure of a Short Story

Objectives

This unit will help you to:

✓ understand the structure of a short story
✓ learn about the story of the English language
✓ vary the length of sentences in your writing
✓ expand your vocabulary : words to do with language

Section A
Guidance

You should by now be becoming more conscious of the specific components of the short story, i.e. structure, characterisation, dialogue, setting and atmosphere. In this and the three following units you will be given more guidance on these components.

When considering the structure of a short story, you need to look at:

- the plot (story-line)

- the angle/point of view

- presentation – the opening and the ending

The plot

How is the story developed? Does it maintain the reader's interest? Is there a punch-line? Does it build to a climax? Is there some unexpected twist?

You can use the three systems, described in Unit 2, to develop your story.

The angle/point of view

Omniscient narrator

The reader is told about the experiences of the characters as if the author were God looking down and seeing everything that goes on.

Narration from the point of view of one character

The story may be presented from the point of view of one character: the reader is made to sympathise with the character, understanding his good points while excusing his bad ones. In a long work (e.g. a novel) there may be shifts from the point of view of one character to another. In each case the character is presented in the third person (i.e. using the pronouns 'he' and 'she').

One of the characters tells the story

A specific person tells the story and this person is presented as 'I', 'me', 'my'. Note, however, that this person does not have to be the main character in the story.

A good author, and you should follow good examples, does not make his characters put forward all his (the author's) own personal beliefs and prejudices. A good author puts himself in the position of the characters by asking 'How would a person like this behave?' 'What would s/he think or say?'

Presentation – the opening

The opening must hold the reader's attention. You can:

- be dramatic

- be mysterious

- be authoritative

- pose a question

Consider, for example, the following openings:

(a)   Ras Ifar was smart, but he had a weakness.

(b)   Did David Balson really commit suicide or was it a freak accident that caused him to drown at the beach yesterday?

(c)   There will be no cure for AIDS before 1999.

(d)   What appeared in the sky last night at twelve o'clock was not a UFO and it was not anything earthly.

In each case curiosity alone will cause the reader to want to read on.

Tears of the sea

Now she spent all her time in the sand pile on the barbecue, pushing deeper and deeper down to watch the sand grains fall, lying down and completely covering herself in the hot sand which rocked her in its cradle until she almost fell asleep. Sometimes when she was lying in the sand and was perfectly relaxed she would feel softly at first, then stronger, a breeze which she knew was coming directly from the sea and she heard in its wake a faint roar, the sound of the sea coming all the way from the coast to where she lay on a barbecue on a mountain top.

And she played games with the shells. She lined them up on the ledge of the barbecue according to shape, to colour, then in order of size. She became a general and they her army, a schoolteacher and they her pupils, a mother and they her numerous children. Each day she found

more and more shells as if they were as endless as the sand grains, bits and pieces of shell, of coral and seafans. And one day she found *the* shell. It was the only one of its kind in the sand pile, in the whole world, she thought, almost a replica of the giant conch shells in the garden, but so tiny it fitted in the palm of her hand and unlike the big conch shells that were bleached white and looked old and worn, this little shell was new and inviting, its deep interior shading to a salmon colour lustre with a touch of mother-of-pearl, its outside ranging from the most delicate pink to gleaming white. It was the most beautiful thing she had ever seen. She immediately knew it was a magic shell sent specially to her as a gift from the sea, and so she was not surprised one day when she held it to her ear to hear first the faint but familiar roar of the ocean and then coming scratchily at first, like the radio, a voice from afar. 'Hello', it said. 'Hello. Hello.' And she finally answered breathless and timid, 'Hello.'

Olive Senior

Exercises

1   What angle/point of view does this story take? What do you think of it as a story opening? Does it make you curious? What do you think happens next?

2   Here are some more openings. Judge for yourself how good they are. Then continue the story by adding fifty more words in each case.

(a)   Colleen stopped running. She couldn't hear the footsteps any longer but she could still feel the hand like a vice around her neck and the hand tearing at her clothes.

(b)   The first time Naomi did it nothing happened. The second time was a different story.

(c)   Son-Son was nervous. This was his first time in the contest. He walked onto the stage and the M.C. handed him the microphone. The crowd went very quiet.

(d)   I couldn't wait for three o'clock. I grabbed my books and ran straight home to tell my mother.

(e)   There is a difference between the front room and the side room. Nobody goes through the front door and nobody comes out the same way they go in.

(f)   On the side of the hill facing the sea the tops of the trees were all at the same level as if a giant lawn mower had cut them.

(g)   My mother was sitting in her chair in the corner and I was watching her out of the corner of my eye to see when she started to nod off.

(h)   Desmond began to believe what the others in the class were saying about Annie. The more he thought about it the more he was convinced it was true.

(i)   I watched the sparrow build the nest, day by day, bit by bit. When she had finished, I took a stick and knocked it down.

(j)   The buses, the cars, the trees and the houses all passed Joseph on his way home. He didn't see any of them. His brain was numb; his hands were cold; his friend was dead.

(k)   We started out at first cock-crow. The grass was wet with dew; it was chilly and it was still dark.

(l)   Lisette was happy. She had passed the exam and was going to go to school in the city. School in the city was a different world altogether.

(m)   Mr Goring went about his morning chores as usual. He cooked his breakfast, took the animals out of their pen and put them around the back. He caught the seven o'clock bus to work and went through the back door into the office. As usual he was the first there, but he didn't see what was on the floor. He couldn't see it and his white cane only knocked it slightly as he passed.

Presentation – the ending

The ending must leave a good or lasting impression on the reader. Good story-tellers often put an unexpected twist into the very last sentence of the story. Some stories have a sudden and happy solution to a very difficult situation. Such a solution is called a *deus ex machina*. However, you do not have to make all stories end unexpectedly or happily.

Assignments   **A**   Get a copy of a daily newspaper and study the headlines for every news item. Explain in each case how the headline attracts you and persuades you to start reading the article. Why is the front page headline important in any newspaper?

B   Divide the class into three groups. Each group will select one of the following topics:

1   An unforgettable incident

2   I was awakened by a loud screaming in the night

3   The accident

Each group will convert the topic into a short realistic sketch (as though from a play). Select a narrator who will make it clear to the audience what is happening.

**Section B
Language
work**

Language: The story of the English language

In about AD 449 a king in part of what is now known as England invited the Angles, the Saxons and the Jutes, Germanic tribes (from what is now Jutland in Denmark and from northern Germany) to help him drive back the Scots and other neighbours to the north. By AD 600 these three tribes had taken over the whole of England, which eventually became known as Engla land (land of the Angles). Each of these three tribes originally had its own Germanic dialect, but in time they combined to become what is called Old English. Old English is more like modern German than it is like modern English.

> (*Thus: Old English = Angle dialect + Jute dialect + Saxon dialect*)

In 1066 England was conquered by the Normans, who came over from France. Because these French-speaking Normans were in control of the government and the Church, their language (which had evolved from Latin) had a profound influence on Old English, which changed to become what is called Middle English. Gradually this Middle English gained ascendancy, so that by 1400 it had replaced French as the language of government and business.

> (*Thus: Middle English = Old English + Norman French*)

By 1500 Middle English had evolved to what is called Modern English, because by that time its structure had become much as it is today. The Modern English period also coincides with European expansion to Africa and the New World and later British colonisation of Australia, India (including Pakistan and Bangladesh), New Zealand and elsewhere. This modern period of English saw the language spread across the whole world, developing its own dialects in each area that it settled. In the sixteenth century there were fewer than two million people who spoke English and they all lived in Britain. Today, more than 450 million people speak English and they live all over the world.

> (*Thus: Modern English = British + American + West Indian + Indian, etc.*)

Sentence composition

Varying the length of sentences

When you first begin to write, you find that you write short sentences. To write well, you need to know how to write sentences of different lengths. However, don't believe that short sentences are bad and long sentences are good. Effective writing requires sentences of all lengths.

You can lengthen your sentences by expanding the subject or the verb or both. Consider the following:

The frightened boy ran away.

The boy, full of fear, ran away.

The boy, with terror written all over his face, ran away.

The boy, seeing death staring him in the face, ran away.

The boy ran away quickly.

The boy ran away with great speed.

The boy ran away as fast as he could.

Exercises   **A**   Rewrite the following, reducing the number of sentences by combining simple sentences. Try to end up with sentences of varying lengths.

1   There were plantations all over the island in the early nineteenth century. They were small but most were well established. None of them had more than one thousand slaves. In all of them hard conditions prevailed. The first noticeable thing was the poor slave huts. There was a big plantation house to the front. This served the white masters. The poor slave huts were off in the back. Many of the slave huts were overcrowded. Six to a room was common. The slaves slept close together on the floor. They slept on coconut fibre or grass. The children slept close together on one side of the hut.

  Most of the animal pens were full. Not only were there cows in them but also pigs and fowls. In addition, horses and mules were kept there. The roads were not paved. They were also narrow. In the dry season they were very dusty.

  In the town there were shops. The shops were made of wood and stone. Some of the shops were painted white. These shops had one or two small rooms at the back. The owners sometimes stayed overnight in these rooms. Tradesmen threw their garbage by the side of the road. Others did so too. Even butchers threw out their refuse to decay and rot in side roads. Disease was widespread. Mosquitoes and flies were all over the place. Malaria, typhoid fever and dysentery took many lives.

2   I usually dislike writing. I particularly dislike writing essays under pressure. My last four written assignments were a history essay, a letter of application, and two research papers for homework. One of the research papers was a five page report. It was prepared for presentation to the class. I had to try to justify a change to co-education in all the schools in the country. The letter of application was addressed to a local electronics firm and requested an interview with the personnel manager.

The letter contained a list of all my qualifications and my achievements in sports. Both the research paper and the letter of application had to be written at short notice, and both involved difficult, although quite different kinds of problems. I really did not like having to write them.

3   The last time I saw Reiza was last month. I was shopping in Georgetown. It was a very hot day, I remember. I met Reiza in Bookers. We were both in the Hardware and General section. I was buying a drill for Tom. It was going to be his birthday the next day. Reiza was buying souvenirs. She told me that they were for her brother. His name is Bernard. He lives in Brooklyn. He was here for a holiday at that time. He was returning the following day. She wanted to give him a present to take home with him. That is why she was buying the souvenirs.

B   After you have done these three exercises get together with another person who did them. Compare yours and his/hers and decide whose versions are better, then ask your teacher to explain whose versions s/he thinks are better and why.

Vocabulary

Expanding your vocabulary

Here are a number of words which are used when talking about language. Study their meanings carefully.

Linguist:	one who studies the structure and function of languages
Dialect:	the language of an area in a country or of a social class
Fluency:	effortless smoothness in speech
Dialogue:	a conversation
Synonyms:	words of similar meaning
Antonyms:	words of opposite meaning
Vocabulary:	the words of a language; a list of words arranged in a certain order
Glossary:	a list of words taken from a text and explained for the benefit of the reader
Viva voce:	by the living voice, oral
Standard:	a variety of the language which is accepted and established as that which should be taught in schools and in which official business should be conducted
Non-standard:	a variety of the language which differs from the standard
Vocal:	pertaining to the voice or to vowels
Aural:	pertaining to the ear
Oral:	pertaining to the mouth
Guttural:	sound produced in the throat
Nasal:	sound produced through the nose

Characterisation

Objectives

This unit will help you to:

✓ describe characters in detail
✓ appreciate the meaning of Standard English
✓ use compound words for describing
✓ make the correct use of the apostrophe

**Section A
Guidance**

Describing characters in detail

Describing your characters in detail helps your reader imagine them; and increases interest in your story.
   To build up a character sketch, think about these questions:

- What does the person look like: face, rest of body, dress, mannerisms?

- How does the person talk: class, opinions, topics of conversation?

- What do others think/say about the character?

- What does the person do for a living?

Exercise

Take a few minutes to study a person. Look at every detail by moving your eyes slowly from top to bottom, from side to side. Use similes and metaphors (see Unit 11) to build up a description, under these headings:

- appearance
- behaviour
- interests
- preferences/hates

- personality
- idiosyncracies
- relationships

Remember to stop, look, listen, describe.

Read the following passage and then identify each characteristic described and how the author describes it in each case.

Old Goriot

His diamonds, gold snuffbox, his chain and personal ornaments disappeared one by one. He had left off his bright blue coat and his whole prosperous-looking outfit, and summer and winter wore an overcoat of coarse chestnut-coloured cloth, a mohair waistcoat, and thick grey, closely-woven breeches. He grew thinner and thinner; his calves were shrunken; his face, once round and beaming with the contentment of a prosperous tradesman, became unusually lined; his forehead grew wrinkled, his jaw prominent. In the fourth year of his life in the Rue Neuve-Sainte-Geneviève he was no longer the same man. The good vermicelli maker who used to look only forty instead of sixty-two, the stout comfortable tradesman, whose face was almost comical in its unsophisticated freshness, whose sprightly bearing had amused and diverted strangers who chanced to meet him in the street, whose smile was still young, now seemed at least seventy and stupid, dull and uncertain. His blue eyes, formerly so lively, seemed to have turned a sad leaden grey; they had faded and dried up and their red rims seemed to ooze blood. People either pitied him or were shocked by him.

Honoré de Balzac

Exercises

1   Make a list of all the adjectives in the passage. Separate the adjectives in lists according to:

sight

touch

other

2   Identify and give examples of all the descriptive structures used by the author. In other words, where do the descriptive words occur in the sentence?

3   How does the author manage to create a clear vision of the character?

Extract from Miguel Street

I first got to know Hat when he offered to take me to the cricket at the Oval. I soon found out that he had picked up eleven other boys from four or five streets around, and was taking them as well.

We lined up at the ticket-office and Hat counted us loudly. He said, 'One and twelve half.'

Many people stopped minding their business and looked up. The man selling tickets said, 'Twelve half?'

Hat looked down at his shoes and said, 'Twelve half.'

We created a lot of excitement when all thirteen of us, Hat at the head, <u>filed around</u> the ground, looking for a place to sit.

People shouted, 'They is all yours, mister?'

Hat smiled, weakly, and made people believe it was so.

When we sat down he made a point of counting us loudly again. He said, 'I don't want your mother raising hell when I get home, saying one missing.'

It was the last day of the last match between Trinidad and Jamaica. Gerry Gomez and Len Harbin were making a great stand for Trinidad, and when Gomez reached his 150 Hat went crazy and danced up and down, shouting, 'White people is God, you hear!'

A woman selling soft drinks passed in front of us.

Hat said, '<u>How</u> you selling this thing you have in the glass and them?'

The woman said, 'Six cents a glass.'

Hat said, 'I want the wholesale price. I want thirteen.'

The woman said, 'These children is all yours?'

Hat said, 'What wrong with that?'

The woman sold the drinks at five cents a glass.

When Len Harbin was 89, he was out lbw, and Trinidad declared.

Hat was angry. 'Lbw? Lbw? How he lbw? Is only a lot of robbery. And is a Trinidad umpire too. God, even umpires taking bribe now.'

Hat taught me many things that afternoon. From the way he pronounced them, I learned about the beauty of cricketers' names, and he gave me all his own excitement at watching a cricket match.

I asked him to explain the scoreboard.

He said, 'On the left-hand side they have the names of the batsman who finish batting.'

I remember that because I thought it such a nice way of saying that a batsman was out: to say that he had finished batting.

All during the tea interval Hat was excited as ever. He tried to get all sorts of people to take all sorts of crazy bets. He ran about waving a dollar-note and shouting, 'A dollar to a shilling, Headley don't reach <u>double figures</u>.' Or, 'A dollar, Stollmeyer field the first ball.'

The umpires were walking out when one of the boys began crying.

Hat said, 'What you crying for?'

The boy cried and mumbled.

Hat said, 'But what you crying for?'

A man shouted, 'He want a bottle.'

Hat turned to the man and said, 'Two dollars, five Jamaican wickets fall this afternoon.'

The man said, 'Is all right by me, if is hurry you is to lose your money.'

A third man held the stakes.

The boy was still crying.

Hat said, 'But you see how you shaming me in front of all these people? Tell me quick what you want.'

The boy only cried. Another boy came up to Hat and whispered in his ear.

Hat said, 'Oh, God! How? Just when they coming out.'

He made us all stand. He marched us away from the grounds and made us line up against the galvanised-iron paling of the Oval.

He said, 'All right, now, pee. Pee quick, all of all-you.'

The cricket that afternoon was fantastic. The Jamaican team, which included the great Headley, lost six wickets for thirty-one runs. In the fading light the Trinidad fast bowler, Tyrell Johnson, was unplayable, and his success seemed to increase his speed.

A fat old woman on our left began screaming at Tyrell Johnson, and whenever she stopped screaming she turned to us and said very quietly, 'I know Tyrell since he was a boy so high. We use to pitch marble together.' Then she turned away and began screaming again.

Hat collected his bet.

This, I discovered presently, was one of Hat's weaknesses – his passion for impossible bets. At the races particularly, he lost a lot of money, but sometimes he won, and then he made so much he could afford to treat all of us in Miguel Street.

V.S. Naipaul

Questions

1   Why did Hat say 'One and twelve half'?

2   Why did Hat 'look down at his shoes' when he said 'Twelve half'?

3   i   Did Hat at any time say that the boys were his children?

    ii   How did Hat create the impression that the boys were his?

4   Why did Hat say 'White people is God'?

5   Why did Hat say 'I want the wholesale price'?

6   What was Hat suggesting when he said, 'God, even umpires taking bribe now'?

7   i What does the author say was one of Hat's weaknesses?

    ii What examples of Hat's weakness are given in the passage?

8   What do you think the boy whispered in Hat's ear?

9   Why did the man shout 'He want a bottle'?

10   What did the 'fat old woman' mean by what she said to the children?

11   Explain fully why 'Hat collected his bet'.

12   Give at least two different reasons to show that Hat was not a mean person.

13   Explain the words and phrases underlined.

14   In one paragraph write a character sketch of Hat. (Do not re-tell the story in the passage.)

Assignment

Each group should select a particular character on whom it will focus.

Develop the appearance of your character, using the following as a guide:

- What kind of face would such a character have – eyes, mouth, nose, etc.?

- What kind of expression would s/he wear?

- Would such a person be short or tall, fat or thin? Why?

- What kinds of mannerisms is this person likely to have?

- How would s/he dress?

Make up one of your group members to look as closely as possible like the particular character. Limited costume, and some make-up, if necessary, may be used.

Develop the speech of your character, using the following as a guide:

- How would such a character speak?

- What kinds of things is s/he likely to say?

Develop the personality of your character, using the following choices as a guide:

reserved – outgoing	domineering – easily led
selfish – generous	vacillating – forthright
silent – talkative	affable – sour
moody – even-tempered	approachable – repulsive

Language: Standard English

Standard English is that form of English which is regarded as correct and appropriate for certain occasions and functions. Correctness and appropriateness are agreed on by educated people but these change as people's judgements change over the centuries. Educated people have come to accept as correct or 'standard' a specific way of spelling English words, a specific way of pronouncing them, and a specific way for punctuation to be used in writing. They have also agreed on what is and what is not a sentence as well as how 'content' words (e.g. apple, dog, run) and 'function' words (e.g. in, as, that) should be used in sentences. All these areas of English which are agreed on and are set out in grammar books and dictionaries constitute Standard English.

However, English is spoken in many parts of the world and the educated people in these countries do not all agree on what is correct or appropriate. For example, Americans and English people disagree on the spelling of some words, but they have *agreed* to disagree, which means that the standard spelling in the USA is not identical to the standard spelling in Britain. There are also differences in words used and in meanings of words from one English-speaking society to another. This means that in addition to those things which are standard for all English speakers, there are things which are standard for individual countries.

Writing has been one of the major forces determining what is standard and what is not. When things are written down, they tend to acquire respectability and more easily become standard. When societies do not have a long history of written literature, there is usually disagreement about whether what is said in those societies is standard or not. This is the case in the West Indies today. There is a tendency in cases like this to regard only what is written down in outside societies (e.g. Britain) as standard and to reject what is local. However, as writing and written literature increase in volume in a society, that society increasingly determines its own standards. So that now, in addition to the already accepted international Standard English, standards of West Indian English are evolving.

Standard English is spoken more widely across the world than any other language. It has become the international language of science and technology. It is also the major language of business and it is one of the official languages of the United Nations. Knowledge of Standard English in today's world therefore is a great advantage. Millions of people over the world are trying to learn English for the economic and social advantages that it gives. It is therefore for reasons of personal and national development that children in the West Indies are required to learn Standard English.

Sentence composition

Compound words used for describing

Certain compounds help you to avoid using too many short sentences with one-word subjects and objects. In these compounds the first part indicates how or with what the thing is done and the second part says what was done. E.g.

hand-made	well-dressed	mass-produced
short-lived	freshly-made	paper-covered
rubber-soled	rain-soaked	horse-drawn

Use these and other such compounds in your essays and stories, but do not overuse them.

Exercises   **A**   Look back to 'Old Goriot' and make a note of any compound describing words you can find there.

B   Move the underlined part in each of the following phrases to a position before the noun, changing its form so that it makes sense and reads well. Then add a part after the noun to make a complete sentence.

Example: The reindeer <u>with the red nose </u>...

Answer: The red-nosed reindeer pulled the sleigh.

1   A boat <u>with a glass bottom</u> ...

2   A secret <u>which has been jealously guarded</u> ...

3   An article <u>which was published rather recently</u> ...

4   A sailor <u>with red eyes</u> ...

5   Attractive houses <u>having two bedrooms</u> ...

6   Cheap production of <u>food for animals</u> ...

7   A dog <u>with teeth like razors</u> ...

8   A paper bag <u>which has stains from grease</u> ...

Punctuation

The apostrophe (')

In nouns the apostrophe is used to indicate possession.

• In singular nouns an **s** is put after the apostrophe. E.g.

the boy's bag, Anne-Marie's bag

- In singular nouns ending with **s** add the apostrophe alone. E.g.

  Mr Jones' car

- In plural nouns ending in **s** add the apostrophe alone after the noun. E.g.

  the boys' bags

- In plural nouns not ending in **s** add **'s**. E.g.

  the sheep's tails, mice's heads

Here is a way to check if you have put the apostrophe in the right place. E.g.

  The girl's shoes   The girls' shoes

Replace the apostrophe or the apostrophe **+ s** by 'of'. Then read backwards:

  'The girl('s) shoes' = shoes of the girl

  The girls(') shoes = shoes of the girls

(*Note*: Children is a plural noun, so the apostrophe is placed before the s.)

  The children's shoes ✔   The childrens' shoes ✗)

Exercise   Using the method of checking given above, analyse:

1   The people's choice

2   The peoples' choice

3   A lady's bag

4   A ladies' bag

The apostrophe in composite nouns – use **'s** once only at the end of the composite noun. E.g.

  The Queen of England's hat

  Bob and Tom's company

  My sister-in-law's brother

  Rosemary's brother-in-law's mother

The apostrophe is used in plurals of letters and figures. E.g.

  Babs got two A's and a B at A-level.

  Roy got three 1's and two 2's at CXC.

The apostrophe is never used in the possessive of pronouns.

my	mine (not mine's)	myself
your	yours	yourself
his	his	himself
her	hers	herself
its	its (not it's)	itself (never it'self)
our	ours	ourselves
your	yours	yourselves
their	theirs	themselves

Exercise

Put the apostrophe in the right place in the following words and phrases.

1   the boys heads

2   the neighbours cat

3   the Prime Minister of Englands house

4   that bag is yours

5   that dog has hurt its leg

6   Mrs Smiths nephews book

7   the teachers meeting

8   John and Anns parents

Dialogue

Objectives

This unit will help you to:

- ✓ learn how to write dialogue
- ✓ understand the meaning of 'non-standard dialect'
- ✓ use a variety of verbs instead of 'get' and 'become'
- ✓ punctuate dialogue correctly

Section A
Guidance

Dialogue in a story

Read the following short extract from a story by the Trinidadian novelist Michael Anthony. After the first reading two students can act out the dialogue.

Extract from
Green days by the river

'Where you was?' he said, 'I was calling you.'

'I was out in the road with Mr Gidharee.'

'Mr who?'

'Mr Gidharee. The man with those big Tobago dogs.'

'You just come up here but you know everybody already.'

' He asked me about you.'

'About me?' He turned round on his side.

'He just asked me if you wasn't working.'

'He have a job for me or what?'

'No, he only ask that. Just so. He want me to go down to his place – you know, a little plantation, like.'

'For what?'

'Don't know.'

'And where's this place?'

'Cedar Grove Road.' I knew he didn't know where that was.

'You better ask your mother,' he said.

I looked at him lying there on the bed and the dougla girl sprang to mind.

'Pa, you remember that dougla girl down in the cafe who showed you up the hill?'

He thought a little and said, 'Aha.'

'That is her father.'

'You mean the Indian man – Gidharee?'

'Yes. Her mother is creole.'

'Oh, I see.'

'He laughed when I called her a dougla.'

'Why? What else you could call her if she's Indian-Creole? It ain't no insult.'

'You don't mean Indian-Creole you mean Indian-Negro.'
I was baiting him now. We had argued on this word creole.
'Okay, Indian-Negro, then,' he said.
'Because creole is –'
'Okay, creole is the foreign settlers, as those silly teachers tell you in school. Anyway that girl is a dougla.'

  His eyes avoided me for a moment because he knew I had won my point. Then he looked at me stealthily and we both laughed.

Michael Anthony

This extract should make you aware that in a story, dialogue is more than just conversation between people; it must serve the function of developing plot or character. What dialogue does most of all, if it is used well and correctly, is to bring the story to life and make it seem more real.

Writing spoken English

The dialogue in a story may be written in Standard English or dialect. Use dialect if you are trying to show something of the social class of your character, or the kind of situation your characters are in. However, before you write any kind of spoken English, read the sections in this unit on 'Language: Non-standard dialect' and 'Punctuation'.

Assignments   **A**   Identify some of the differences between dialect in your country and Standard English.

B   Ask an older person (grandparent, older relative or acquaintance) to tell you a story. Write this story in your own words. Each student should present his/her short story and the teacher together with the class will select the three best.

Section B Language work

Language: Non-standard dialect

In every society in contrast to the standard form of the language, there are other ways of pronouncing words and there are expressions as well as words that are used by smaller groups within the society. For instance, you may be able to identify people from a parish or county by their pronunciation, or you may be able to identify persons because they use 'uneducated' speech almost all the time. All such differences within a language are called dialectal differences, and identifiable ways of producing the language are called 'dialects' of the language. Dialects, therefore, are directly connected to parts of the country and also to social classes in the society.

In the West Indies in particular Standard English stands in contrast to the variety of language which most people grow up speaking normally. This native speech is usually called 'the dialect' and results from the circumstances in which European languages (English in our case) were learnt in the West Indies. Many people think of this native speech as 'broken' English.

All dialects of a language which contrast with the standard are referred to as 'non-standard'. The major difference between standard and non-standard is that the former has more prestige than the latter. On the other hand, the native dialect is dear to one's heart because it captures deep-seated emotions and feelings powerfully and directly. In addition, non-standard dialect can reveal much information about the place of birth, the social class, the character and outlook of the speaker. Non-standard dialect is therefore an integral part of short stories in the West Indies.

Sentence composition

Verbs of 'becoming'

'Get' is colloquial and informal. It is a useful word because it can fit into almost any spot where you want to give the meaning 'become'. The word 'become' is also popular but it is not used as frequently as 'get' because it is not as informal or casual. However, you should try to expand your active vocabulary and give your speech and writing more style. Here are a few other words that can be used instead of 'get' and 'become':

> *grow turn fall run go wear come*

grow	The sick person grew stronger. As he grew older ...
turn	Leaves turn brown and mangoes turn ripe. White people turn pale.
fall	People fall sick.
run	Children/fields run wild. Rivers, wells, taps run dry.
go	Food goes bad.
wear	My patience is wearing thin.
come	Everything comes right at the end.

Some of these verbs are used in informal speech in some territories in the West Indies in a way that differs from the way in which they are used in International English. Note the following

(W.I. = West Indian English; I.E. = International English):

W.I.   The room came hot as a furnace.
I.E.   The room became as hot as a furnace.

W.I.   When I turn a big woman ...
I.E.   When I grow up ... /When I become a grown woman ...

W.I.   When I grow a big man ...
I.E.   When I grow up / When I am a man ...

W.I.   As she turned sixteen ...
I.E.   As soon as she was sixteen ...

Exercise

Paying specific attention to the underlined words, give a more formal Standard English equivalent to ten of the following sentences. You can rearrange the sentences if you have to.

1   <u>How</u> are you selling the potatoes?

2   The old woman <u>raised</u> her daughter's children.

3   She is <u>to call him uncle.</u>

4   The boys were <u>skylarking</u> in the classroom.

5   He can be very <u>ignorant</u> sometimes.

6   It was my father who <u>learned</u> me to drive.

7   She likes to <u>fast</u> in people's business.

8   He is too <u>forward.</u>

9   I will be able to tell you tomorrow <u>bar(ring)</u> I don't see him.

10   You are <u>taking advantage of</u> the girl.

11   I would give it to the dog <u>before</u> I give it to you.

12   <u>Being</u> I was there, he didn't do anything.

13   <u>Through</u> Beenie didn't come to school, I couldn't come.

14   <u>From</u> I was a child, I have never liked going to see my aunt.

15   My sister <u>favour</u> me and both of us favour our mother.

16   <u>Take care</u> you <u>mash</u> my foot.

17   The things <u>catch</u> me to my waist.

18   She used whatever <u>convenience</u> she had to catch the water.

19   When I got there a <u>whole heap of</u> people were there already.

20   He was there <u>betwixt and between</u>.

21   This boy is too <u>hard-ears</u>.

22   He has been <u>two-timing</u> his girl-friend for a long time now.

23   He promised to <u>look in</u> on the old lady tomorrow.

24   She <u>cut her eye at</u> me, but I didn't <u>pay her any mind</u>.

Punctuation

Punctuating speech or dialogue

When punctuating speech, you first of all have to make a clear distinction between what a person actually says and what you or anyone else says that the person said. E.g.

Actual speech – 'I am eating.'

Reported speech = what you or anyone else says that the person said: He is telling you that he is eating.

Points to remember

- The actual words are separated from the rest – this is done by putting them within quotation marks. E.g.

'I am eating,' he said.

(You may use single quotation marks or double quotation marks. Whichever you choose, remember to keep on using them throughout.)

- The first word of actual speech, wherever it is in the sentence, begins with a capital letter. E.g.

He shouted to me, 'Your brother is eating.'

- For each new speaker begin on a new line, in the same way that you would start a new paragraph.

- There are particular rules for using commas, colons, full stops, question marks and exclamation marks in writing direct speech/dialogue.

Use a comma before words in quotation marks if the quotation marks begin in the middle of the sentence. E.g.

John said, 'I am eating.'

Sometimes you will see a colon used instead, especially in dialogue. E.g.

John said: 'I am eating.'

Mary: 'Let's go now.'

Jane: 'No, not now. It's too late.'

Mary: 'No, it isn't. We still have time.'

Jane: 'Well, alright then.'

If the quoted words come first in the sentence, put the comma, full stop, question mark or exclamation mark inside the quotation mark. E.g.
'I am eating,' John said.

'I am eating!' John exclaimed.

'Am I eating?' John asked.

Exercises   **A**   Which is the correctly punctuated sentence in each group?

1   (i)   Arthur asked me if I was going riding today?
      (ii)   Arthur asked me, if I was going riding today.
      (iii) Arthur asked me, 'If I was going riding today?'
      (iv)   Arthur asked me if I was going riding today.

2   (i)   Prisoners who haven't completed their tasks, will receive no concessions.
      (ii)   Prisoners, who haven't completed their tasks will receive no concessions.
      (iii) Prisoners who haven't completed their tasks will receive no concessions.
      (iv)   Prisoners, who hav'ent completed their tasks, will receive no concessions.

3   (i)   "Bambi" is silly,' he said. 'It's a little children's movie.'
      (ii)   'Bambi is silly,' he said, It's a little childrens' movie.'
      (iii) Bambi is silly. He said, it's a little children's movie.
      (iv)   'Bambi' is silly, he said. Its a little childrens movie.

4   (i)   Players selected from whom no dues have been received, will not be allowed to play.
      (ii)   Players selected, from whom no dues have been received will not be allowed to play.
      (iii) Players selected from whom no dues have been received will not be allowed to play.
      (iv)   Players selected, from whom no dues have been received, will not be allowed to play.

B   Punctuate the following passages and insert all necessary capital letters.

1   a very worried man arrived one evening at the doctor please doctor he said you must help me what is the problem said the doctor well said the man as i stop speaking i completely forget what ive been talking about i see said the doctor and how long has this been going on how long has what been going on said the man

2   john jacob thomas was an unusual trinidadian who lived in the second half of the nineteenth century the son of ex slaves of african descent educated in a public elementary school he was a schoolteacher and then a civil servant but his interests were literary and he was the author of creole grammar a study of trinidad patois thomas main interest was in language and it was in the villages where he taught that he had developed his linguistic talents becoming fluent in english french and creole and beginning a study of spanish in 1869 he completed creole grammar a study of the french derived creole patois spoken by most trinidadians in the nineteenth century it was his first effort in print and perhaps his most remarkable in later years he described how he came to write it the preface to creole grammar states that its author turned his attention to our popular patois for the purpose of ascertaining its exact relation to real french his research suffered from a lack of books there were none at all on creole and he had very few on french but thomas was also a philologist of the more academic type interested in creole as a linguistic phenomenon illustrating the derivative process he saw creole as a direct descendant of french as spoken by african slaves with additions to the vocabulary from african languages english spanish and amerindian dialects

Objectives

This unit will help you to:

- ✓ provide an interesting setting and atmosphere for your story
- ✓ understand the development of West Indian English
- ✓ know the rules concerning noun and verb agreement
- ✓ practise choosing the word closest in meaning to another

Section A
Guidance

Thinking about the setting

When you are thinking about the setting for your story, use the following as a guide:

- In what kind of scene or setting do you think the incidents in your story are likely to occur?

- If the atmosphere is a frightening one, what kinds of things do you think are likely to make it frightening?
  What kinds of noises?

- If the atmosphere is tense, what could add to the tension (clock? time ticking by?) When you watch a story on television, listen to the background music and noise and see how it heightens tension.

- If the scene has changed from being a happy one to a sad one, then how was it obvious in the first place that it was happy; how is it obvious that it is now sad?

Read the following passages from Edgar Mittelholzer and answer the questions after each one.

Extract from
West Indian
Stories (1)

It was an afternoon of grey clouds like old rice bags, and the wind strong and loud in its moaning, so loud that on the back veranda where Harry, Hoolcharran's third son, sat in a bright-blue wicker chair the voices in the house could not be heard. The wind smelt of cow-dung and stagnant water and the iodine of the sea, for the savannah surrounded the house on all sides, and parts of the savannah were flooded from the rains of last week, and on the dry parts <u>small island-cakes of cow-dung lay spotted: still, piteous islands amid the larger islands that moved</u>, for these were the cows and sheep and the goats. Now and then the wind brought a lowing or a bleating, or the voice of a herdsman, for this was the hour when the animals were coming home to their pens, and it was the hour, too, when Hoolcharran, who owned them all and the house, was dying.

Exercises

1   List the descriptive words and phrases according to the senses of sight, hearing and smell. How does the author try to get the reader to identify specific smells?

2   Look up the words 'pathetic fallacy' in your dictionary. Discuss how this term may be applied to this passage, paying specific attention to the very last word in the passage.

3   Explain the metaphorical language in the part <u>underlined</u> and say what kind of setting the author is trying to create.

(See Unit 11, page 100 on how metaphor is used in poetry.)

Extract from *West Indian Stories* (2)

'It was a horrible, slouching thing that was with him,' she told us. 'It was daytime, but the foliage overhead threw everything into a kind of twilight, though I could still make the thing out clearly. It had grey, wettish limbs – limbs like flippers – and there was a kind of fur on its body. And it had a squashed-in head with two spaces like eye-sockets. They looked blue very blue. Ugh! And – and while Mynheer Voorman kept pleading and whimpering and beseeching me to help him dig up the bones and things this horrible creature squirmed and staggered about. It seemed afraid of something in the air around it. It made queer scratching noises – or scraping noises – and it thumped about, and at one moment I saw something flicker like fire near it, and it seemed to

57

break apart into slimy rags – but it came together again. And then after a while there was a big white flash, and it snarled and sprang at me. I smelt that foul, musky smell, and I heard it rasp out something at me. It was the same voice I used to hear in my other dreams. It used English words, and it said distinctly:

'Seven more hours – and he and you will join us forever and forever!' And it gave a kind of slobbering squeak, and I felt it press something against my hip – something clammy and hard. I couldn't see what it was, but I knew it was a flute. It branded me – branded me as that woman up the river was branded.'

Edgar Mittelholzer

Exercises

1   List all the descriptive words and phrases the author uses to describe the creature and then say which of the senses the author is concentrating on.

2   Are the many descriptive words and phrases used to give you a clear picture or to create an impression?
Give reasons for your answer.

3   What do you think the last sentence means?

Assignment

Set the scene for

• the opening of a murder trial of a well-known person

• a walk through a graveyard in the dead of night

• waiting for a big raffle or race to take place

Section B Language work

Language: The story of West Indian English

The English language was brought to the West Indies by people from England, Ireland, Scotland and Wales who came to settle in the colonies. The earliest of these colonists first settled in Barbados and St Kitts from about the 1620s and from these two islands spread to the other territories. Africans were brought mainly from the coastal areas of West Africa (the area that stretches from Senegal, through Sierra Leone and Liberia to Nigeria) and had to learn the English which they heard from the English speakers with whom they came into contact.

The English, Irish, Scottish and Welsh colonists and later bondservants spoke different dialects of English and were generally of the lower class and uneducated. There was no such thing in England at the time of the early settlement as Standard English which was widely known, looked up to, spoken and written by the general population, for it was not until 1707 that England, Ireland, Scotland and Wales actually became one country. The slaves therefore heard and learnt by word of mouth words, expressions, grammatical constructions, and pronunciations of various dialects of English, which were in many respects different from what has become Standard English of today.

The West Africans, who already had their own languages, had to learn a foreign language quickly and in very unfavourable conditions. The English they spoke was greatly affected by their own languages, and so the creole languages developed. The amount of English the Africans learnt was governed by their social status. Those (the house slaves) who were in close association with English speakers learnt a lot more than those who worked in the fields, away from the whites.

When the East Indians came from different parts of India to the West Indies during the nineteenth century, they not only learnt the creole languages but also kept their own languages. However, because East Indians have continued to come to the West Indies over the years, not all of them have learnt the creole languages. The East Indians have added several words to the local dialects, especially in Trinidad and Guyana.

The process of learning more and more English has never stopped and today fewer people speak the creole languages and more people speak dialects that are closer to English. However, English in the West

Indies is heavily influenced by the creole languages and it contains meanings, expressions, pronunciations and structures which are not found in English in other parts of the world. In addition, since each territory has its own history and development, the English in each territory is different.

Sentence composition

Subject–verb agreement

The rule to remember is: A verb agrees with its subject in number.

- If the subject is singular, the verb is also singular.

- If the subject is plural, the verb is plural.

Expanded sentences often create problems as far as making the subject agree with the verb is concerned. Take the following sentence:

> The man with two wives was convicted.

Should the verb be 'was' or 'were'?

The correct form is 'was' (singular) because the subject of the sentence is 'man' (singular). The phrase with two wives is only an expansion of the subject. The structure of the sentence is therefore:

> The *man* with two wives *was* convicted.

However, it is a very common error to make the main verb agree with the noun nearest to it, instead of with the subject. You can avoid this error by identifying in every sentence the verb and the subject and making sure that they agree.

More difficult cases occur in the following examples:

> The *first* of the trucks is here.

> A *bowl* of beans is on the table.

> The *sins* of the father have been visited upon the son.

In each case the italicised word is really the subject; in each case the phrase following 'of the trucks', 'of beans', 'of the father' is just like 'with two wives' above, i.e. an expansion of the subject. Do not be misled by what seems to be the meaning; the real subject will hardly ever occur after 'of', 'with', 'by'.

When 'and' joins two or more singular nouns or pronouns the subject is plural. E.g.

> The boy and the girl are here.

> You and I were there.

Note that 'and' often has the same meaning as 'with' or 'accompanied by' or 'along with' but in subject–verb agreement they are treated differently. E.g.

John and his sister (plural) are outside.

John (singular), together with his sister, is outside.

John (singular), accompanied by his sister, is outside.

John (singular), along with his sister, is outside.

Exercise

Where necessary correct the following sentences.

1   The marks on his face indicates his tribe.

2   Because she likes the excitement, Cyndi, along with her group, go to wrestling all the time.

3   At last, a good use for old tyres are being discovered.

4   Finally, man's belief that his own desires, at least in part, control his future are being realised.

5   Either the cyclists or the truck were to blame.

6   Everyone shirk their duty sometimes.

7   There has always been large numbers of Chinese living in the USA.

8   A significant number of East Indians was living in Trinidad by the 1880s.

9   In the Caribbean, the effects of British colonialism is still being felt.

10   If she want an abortion, she should get it.

11   Language vary from place to place and from class to class.

12   There are a pair of your mother's shoes under the bed.

13   The two most important of these is escape from reality and the need to belong.

14   Mumps are dangerous in the case of young men.

15   One of the main reasons why young people are better informed about sex than their parents were are that they get a lot of information from television.

16   The problems of changing the system is too great for one group or association.

17   The only thing that is certain is taxes and death.

18   Is it Times Store or the other shop that carry that line?

Singular subjects

Those nouns which look plural (because they end in 's') but have a singular meaning are followed by singular verbs. E.g.

mathematics   physics

Subjects which are made up of two nouns which go together in a familiar way are followed by a singular verb. E.g.

Ham and eggs is what I had for breakfast.

Whisky and soda is your drink, but rum and coke is mine.

Sums of money, periods of time and numbers are followed by singular verbs. E.g.

Two dollars is too much to pay for that.

Ten weeks is not the normal length of a term.

Twelve is not the right number.

The words 'none', 'every', 'everybody', 'everyone' are followed by singular verbs. E.g.

None of the videos was working.

Every blade of grass is going to be removed.

Everyone in the class believes that everybody else is bright.

Plural subjects

Errors in subject–verb agreement are often made when people do not realise that some words are plural and not singular. In English not all plural nouns end in 's' or 'es'. There are five words which are commonly used by educated people so often in the plural and so seldom in the singular that the singular form is not well known. As a result of this the plural form is misused as the singular. These five words are:

Plural	*Singular*
media	medium
data	datum
strata	stratum
phenomena	phenomenon
criteria	criterion

Here are a few more 'um' singular, 'a' plural words:

erratum errata:	a typological error in a book which is acknowledged by the author
addendum addenda:	meaning a part added to the main part of a book, report, document
memorandum memoranda:	meaning a note or reminder or special type of business letter.

Words which can be either singular or plural

Some words which have a plural ending ('s') can be either singular or plural in meaning. E.g.

Statistics are figures, but statistics is a subject.

Certain collective nouns, e.g. 'team', 'group', 'crowd', may be used sometimes to mean the group as a whole and sometimes the group as a number of individuals. When 'group as a whole' is intended, use a singular verb following; when 'group as a number of individuals' is intended, use a plural verb following.

The word 'number' is followed by a singular verb if it has 'the' in front of it. E.g.

The number of people present is small.

The word 'number' is followed by a plural verb if it has 'a' in front. E.g.

A number of people were dancing in the hall.

Exercise

In each of the following sentences identify the correct form of the verb.

1   I know that mathematics always bother/bothers my brother.

2   Either the accountant or the financial controller is/are the culprit.

3   The number of people outside the stands was/were the cause of the tragedy.

4   If the committee do/does not submit the decisions, we cannot make plans for the festival.

5   The jury was/were not all in agreement with the verdict.

6   A majority of voters do/does not vote in most elections.

7   The members of the board of management is/are appointed by the President.

8   The crew of the plane was/were supposed to eat different meals at different places.

9   I know that none of the players want/wants to play the match tomorrow.

10   Most of the coins was/were recovered, but two was/were still missing.

Vocabulary

Exercise

In each case below choose out of i, ii, iii, iv the word that is closest in meaning to the word underlined in the sentence:

1   Their views were quite divergent.

    i different   ii diametrically opposite

    ii parallel   iv radical

2   He was the most conscientious worker in the factory.

    i   caring   iii honest

    ii hardworking   iv loyal

3   After the robbery the police noticed that the safe was intact.

    i   open   iii untouched

    ii damaged   iv marked

4   Breaking stones with a hammer is tedious work.

    i   harmful   iii everlasting

    ii tiresome   iv boring

5   The Carnival Queen was beautiful and vivacious.

    i   glamorous   iii lively

    ii photogenic   iv sexy

6   The weatherman says that there will be occasional showers.

    i   frequent   iii light

    ii infrequent   iv brief

7   The boy was now faced with a dilemma.

    i   tragedy   iii choice

    ii challenge   iv difficult choice

8   There have always been arguments whether any of the West Indian countries have homogeneous populations.

    i   easily ruled iii very intelligent

    ii uniform   iv brainwashed

9   After he was elected he showed himself to be very vindictive.

    i   revengeful   iii biased

    ii cruel   iv prejudiced

Making a Story Come Alive

Objectives

This unit will help you to:
- ✓ write a lively story
- ✓ understand how writers' styles vary
- ✓ appreciate how some verbs have objects and some do not
- ✓ use local words correctly
- ✓ memorise the correct spelling of words

Section A Guidance

Making your story come alive

The work you have done in Units 3–6, on the components of the short story, will help you write good stories.

Remember the components:

- structure
- characterisation
- dialogue
- setting and atmosphere

However to make your story come alive you need to:

- be creative
- be interesting
- be vivid

A dull and predictable story is like a stale joke – it is boring.

One way to be creative is to tell a familiar story from an unusual point of view. For example, you can tell a story about 'A day at the beach' from the point of view of the sea (i.e. as if the sea could see, feel, hear, etc.) or about 'An accident' from the point of view of one of the vehicles involved.

To make your story interesting try to present the events in a way that the reader cannot tell what will happen next. Try to think of a punch-line or statement which takes the reader by surprise or is so outstanding that it causes the reader to remember the story.

To be vivid practise describing in detail; do not dwell on obvious details. Use adjectives of colour, texture, smell or taste (e.g. 'a pot-bellied brown man with eyes like cricket balls'). Use adverbs to describe how things happened (e.g. 'quickly', 'noisily'). Use similes of your own; avoid hackneyed ones. (See Unit 11, page 99 on how simile is used in poetry.)

Read the extract on the next page and answer the questions that follow.

Extract from *The old man and the sea*

The old man was sweating now but from something else besides the sun. On each calm placid turn the fish made he was gaining line and he was sure that in two turns more he would have a chance to get the harpoon in.

But I must get him close, close, close, he thought. I mustn't try for the head. I must get the heart.

'Be calm and strong, old man,' he said.

On the next circle the fish's back was out but he was a little too far from the boat. On the next circle he was still too far away but he was higher out of water and the old man was sure that by gaining some more line he could have him alongside.

He had rigged his harpoon long before and its coil of light rope was in a round basket and the end was made fast to the bitt in the bow.

The fish was coming in on his circle now calm and beautiful-looking and only his great tail moving. The old man pulled on him all that he could to bring him closer. For just a moment the fish turned a little on his side. Then he straightened himself and began another circle.

'I moved him,' the old man said. 'I moved him then.'

He felt faint again now but he held on the great fish all the strain that he could. I moved him, he thought. Maybe this time I can get him over. Pull, hands, he thought. Hold up, legs. Last for me, head. Last for me. You never went. This time I'll pull him over.

But when he put all of his effort on, starting it well out before the fish came alongside and pulling with all his strength, the fish pulled part way over and then righted himself and swam away.

'Fish,' the old man said. 'Fish, you are going to have to die anyway. Do you have to kill me too?'

That way nothing is accomplished, he thought. His mouth was too dry to speak but he could not reach for the water now. I must get him alongside this time, he thought. I am not good for many more turns. Yes you are, he told himself. You're good for ever.

On the next turn, he nearly had him. But again the fish righted himself and swam slowly away.

You are killing me, fish, the old man thought. But you have a right to. Never have I seen a greater, or more beautiful, or a calmer or more noble thing than you, brother. Come on and kill me. I do not care who kills who.

Now you are getting confused in the head, he thought. You must keep your head clear. Keep your head clear and know how to suffer like a man. Or a fish, he thought.

'Clear up, head,' he said in a voice he could hardly hear. 'Clear up.'

Twice more it was the same on the turns.

I do not know, the old man thought. He had been on the point of feeling himself go each time. I do not know. But I will try it once more.

He tried it once more and he felt himself going when he turned the fish. The fish righted himself and swam off again slowly with the great tail weaving in the air.

I'll try it again, the old man promised, although his hands were mushy now and he could only see well in flashes.

He tried it again and it was the same. So, he thought, and he felt himself going before he started; I will try it once again.

He took all his pain and what was left of his strength and his long gone pride and he put it against the fish's agony and the fish came over on to his side and swam gently on his side, his bill almost touching the planking of the skiff, and started to pass the boat, long, deep, wide, silver and barred with purple and interminable in the water.

The old man dropped the line and put his foot on it and lifted the harpoon as high as he could and drove it down with all his strength, and more strength he had just summoned, into the fish's side just behind the great chest fin that rose high in the air to the altitude of the man's chest. He felt the iron go in and he leaned on it and drove it further and then pushed all his weight after it.

E. Hemingway

Questions

1 Say in one short sentence what happens in the passage.

2 Describe the character of the old man. What emotional changes does the old man go through in the passage?

3 Why do you think the old man talks to himself? Why does the author use direct speech in the passage?

4 Where is the action taking place? Why does the author not concentrate on setting and atmosphere?

5 The author relies on 'but' and 'and' to connect sentences. What effect does this have on his style?

Assignment

Choose one of the following titles and write a short story, remembering all the advice you have been given in this and previous units:

- The day I shall never forget

- Lost child

- Adventure at the beach

Section B Language work

Language: An author's style

The likes and dislikes of a writer, his/her preference for saying things one way as opposed to another, his/her choice of some words and avoidance/ignorance of others, all these make up the author's style. Style is the way in which a writer uses language to achieve his/her purpose.

You can compare style in language to style in any game. Take, for example, a batsman hitting a four in cricket: he may 'caress' the ball to the boundary; he may 'cuff' it to the boundary; he may hit it 'savagely/brutally' to the boundary, or he may 'mishit' it to the boundary. The number of runs scored in each case is the same, but the manner and reactions caused are different. The same applies to a player scoring a goal in any sport. The same applies to the many different ways one piece of basic information can be communicated to others.

Inexperienced writers are often so limited in their choices that they do not seem conscious of the idea of choosing between different ways of saying things. Experienced writers, on the other hand, are conscious of many ways of saying the same thing and for the most part choose specific words and sentence structures consciously. You can see conscious choices by experienced writers as they move from rough draft (to second and other drafts) to fair copy. Because people's likes and dislikes do not suddenly change drastically, a writer's overall style tends to remain the same and to be familiar and identifiable after a certain time, in the same way that a ball-player tends to play with the same style game after game.

Sentence composition

Verbs with objects and verbs without objects

(noun + verb + noun)   (noun + verb)

Some verbs have a noun following. E.g. 'Anne likes mangoes.' Some verbs do not have a noun following. E.g. 'The dog is sleeping.'

Some English verbs like 'burst', 'break' and 'ring' are versatile – sometimes they have a noun following and sometimes they don't. E.g.

The balloon burst. (noun + verb)

The cat burst the balloon. (noun + verb + noun)

The glass broke. (noun + verb)

The cat broke the glass. (noun + verb + noun)

The school bell is ringing. (noun + verb)

The sexton rang the church bell. (noun + verb + noun)

Other verbs of this type are 'smoke', 'burn', 'change', 'cook'.

Exercise

Say which of the following eighteen sentences are correct in Standard English. Change those which are not to make them correct.

1   Eggs are selling well nowadays.

2   The cricket match will resume after the rest day.

3   The wooden house was old and quickly burnt to the ground.

4   The car will advertise in the newspaper tomorrow.

5   My brother's uncle died yesterday and he will bury on Thursday.

6   If you name Oliver, I name Oliver too.

7   Slave trading stations had already set up there.

8   It is very easy for the egg of a bird to fall and crush.

9   The first session of the Caricom Ministers' Conference will hold on Monday in St Lucia.

10   Man is going to destroy for his sins. You mark my word.

11   Tickets are selling at the box office from 9 am to 4 pm.

12   My school is the Roseau Combined School. It painted green and beige.

13   'School just called. The school bell just rang'.

14   The nurse said that if everything went well, the vaccination would take.

15   That wire can bend.

16   The sand is washing away.

17   Jones was born in the Bahamas, where he trained as a teacher before going to England in 1979.

18   I am going to win first prize in the raffle which is drawing on Thursday.

Some tricky verbs

There are some tricky verbs in English which overlap and cause confusion but they have to be clearly separated. E.g.

- 'lie' takes no noun after it but 'lay' does, so:

    'The dog is lying there.' but 'Hens lay eggs.'

- 'fall' takes no noun after it but 'fell' does , so:

    'The book fell.' but 'He felled the tree.'

- 'rise' takes no noun after it but 'raise' does, so:

    'Birds rise early.' but 'He raised the bar.'

Exercise

Make up three correct sentences of your own for each of the previous verbs.

Vocabulary

When writing short stories, you may have to mention the plants, animals, festivals, superstitions, foods and customs of your own neighbourhood or country. One problem may be that you never have seen these words in print. Also you may not be sure whether the words you use are 'good' words. Your solution may be to avoid all local words and to use only those you believe are 'good'.

On the other hand, you may use words and not realise that the meaning they have for you is not the meaning they have for other people. Take, for instance, the words 'beverage', 'operation', 'surgery'. In some territories the common usage and meaning are different from Standard English.

No self-respecting teacher or examiner will want you to avoid the things with which you are familiar and which are a part of your culture. In fact, you are encouraged to write about yourself and your country. It would help you if you could read as many West Indian short stories and novels as possible to see how the authors use those words with which you are familiar . This will be a good guide for you when you have to write short stories.

Local words add colour and vividness to descriptions, allowing the reader to visualise the scenes and incidents more clearly. At the same time, however, you should not use too many local words whose meanings are known only within a small community, simply because the reader will be put off and will not constantly stop to decipher the meaning.

Points to remember

• Choose your words carefully.

• Do the words get over what you want to say?

• Can the reader understand what you are saying?

Exercises

Following are some West Indian words.

1   Select five of them and explain their meaning to a person visiting from New Zealand.

2   Identify those words which are normally used in your country. Find out where the others are from and what they mean.

3   Write a story of about 200 words using in a sensible way as many of the words as possible.

diablesse	ackee	sorrel
baccoo	calaloo	mountain dew
soucouyant	bakes	yam
mama glo	funji	dasheen
papa bois	bammy	limbo
dwen	float	shango
ligarou	johnny cake	parang
mermaid	pone	bacchanal
rolling calf	sweet-bread	dip and fall back
duppy	steak fish	
jumbee	pelau	

Spelling

How to improve your memory

There are two basic ways your memory improves – the first is by constant repetition and the second is by association. Constant repetition can be reinforced by writing. When you are not sure of the spelling of a word, look it up in the dictionary, spell it out and, in addition, write it down anywhere. Writing it down will help your memory. Remember, however, that looking up a word in a dictionary ONCE, spelling it out ONCE and writing it down ONCE does not mean that you will remember it FOREVER.

With words which you find difficult to spell try associating them with other words or other things. This is called *mnemonics*, which means 'the art of assisting the memory'. For example, if you are not sure whether 'benefit' or 'benifit' is the correct spelling, try to remember that 'bene' is the first part of a number of words, e.g. 'benediction', 'benefit', 'benevolence'.

If you have trouble spelling 'seize' and 'siege', it may be easy first to remember that the two are different i.e. one has 'ei' and the other 'ie'. Remember 'seize' as 'se – ize' = see – eyes or see – i's. This would indicate that, in this instance, 'e' comes before 'i' – therefore 'seize'. This, then, should help you remember that siege is the opposite.

Three tips to better spelling:

- When in doubt use a word which you can definitely spell rather than using a more impressive word which you may spell wrongly.

- Pause a while before you write down everyday familiar sayings or current expressions – the exact spelling of these expressions may be quite different from what you think.

- The verb forms of English are varied and complicated – there is no short-cut or simple rule that will cover all the complexities of English.

Exercise

Make a list of ten words which you find difficult to spell correctly. Look up the correct spelling in a dictionary. Devise a method for remembering the correct spelling. Work on them in the course of one week, then ask a friend to test you. The next week, make yourself a new list.

Different Tones of Voice

Objectives

This unit will help you to:

✓ understand how authors use different techniques to vary the tone of their writing
✓ look for ambiguities in writing
✓ choose the most appropriate word in a variety of sentences
✓ use punctuation correctly to link and enclose parts of your writing

Section A Guidance

A very important feature of any piece of writing is its tone; this determines in large measure how the reader will react. Tone is the attitude of the writer towards either his audience or towards what he is writing about.

One of the earliest things you come to understand when you learn your language as a child is the tone of voice of a speaker. If a person says, for example, 'Laurence is coming' you can tell from the person's 'tone of voice' whether the person is serious or joking, whether the person is afraid, annoyed or excited, whether the person believes what he/she is saying or not. The speaker's tone of voice tells you his/her attitude towards what s/he is saying and towards the people and things involved. For example, a speaker can be:

- sincere

- cynical

- sarcastic

- ironic or satirical

Although it is normal for people to interpret tone correctly in actual speech, in writing it is much more difficult, because the inflections of the voice cannot be converted into writing.

Your attitude or tone should always be appropriate for the subject matter you are writing and for your audience. You also need to understand and remember the words that are used to describe and identify different tones, e.g. cynicism, sarcasm, irony, and satire.

Cynicism

This is an expression of doubt and mistrust of the motives and behaviour of others. You may want to use the word 'cynical' to describe somebody who seems unnecessarily anti-social. The words 'pessimistic' and 'sceptical' also involve doubt and lack of trust. You use 'pessimistic' to describe someone who seems not to be able to help being negative; you use 'sceptical' to describe someone who seems to have some justifiable reason for not believing too easily.

Sarcasm

This is an intention to hurt someone by making remarks which show scorn, contempt, ridicule. It is usually done by an indirect method, i.e. either saying the opposite to what you mean or by understatement or by seeming to speak to several people when your remarks are meant for one specific person. The word sarcastic can be used to describe a person who has a habit of making such remarks or to describe a specific remark. It is used more often to refer to speech than to writing.

Irony

This is saying the opposite of what is meant; the tone of voice or context allows the hearer to interpret the correct meaning. The word 'ironic' can also be used to describe an event or result that is the opposite of what is naturally expected. 'Ironic' is not normally used to describe the person speaking, but what is said or how it is said.

Satire

This is the ridiculing of human behaviour, i.e. people's habits, beliefs, customs, ideas. It is found in writing (i.e. thought out, even if later spoken) more than spontaneous speech. It is not usually used to refer to an isolated comment, but a series of comments, a speech, a poem, a novel, a calypso, cartoons, comic strips, paintings, movies, plays. A satirist is a person who produces satires.

In this calypso the Mighty Sparrow, by quoting from a speech and imitating the behaviour of a former Prime Minister of Trinidad and Tobago, is poking fun at him. Many calypsos are satirical.

Solomon

I am going to bring back Solomon
Who don't like it, complain to the Commission
None of them going tell me how to run my country
I defy anyone of you to dictate for me
I am no dictator, but when I pass an order
Mr Speaker, this matter must go no further
I have nothing more to say
And it must be done my way
Come on, come on, come on, meeting done for the day
This land is mine, I am the boss
What I say goes and who vex loss

I say that Solomon will be Minister of External Affair
If you ain't like it, get to hell outa here

I am going to do what I feel to do
And I couldn't care less who vex or who get blue ...
Who give you the privilege to object?
Pay you' taxes, shut up and have respect
I'm a tower of strength, yes
I'm powerful but modest ... unless
I'm forced to be blunt and ruthless
So shut up and don't squawk
This ain't no skylark
When I talk, no damn dog bark
My word is law so watch you' case
If you slip you slide, this is my place.

And I say that Solomon will be Minister of External Affair
And if you ain't like it, get to hell outa here.

Mighty Sparrow

Assignment

By looking at newspapers and magazines, and by listening to the radio, collect further examples of satire. They may be in the form of calypsos, or cartoons.

The two passages which follow give further examples of how writers can vary their tone of voice.

Extract from *The setting sun and the rolling world*

A man carrying a packet of tomatoes was knocked down by a car as he was crossing Cripps Road. He travelled in the air for twenty feet before he dropped to the side of the road. No one actually saw him hit.

He fell on his left side and face and did not move. His thigh was broken and twisted under him so that the foot faced backwards. His left arm lay twisted under him and the right was flung out backwards, palm up, as if he was asking for something. His grey socks had holes in them through which his yellow toes showed. One shoe lay on its side near his head. A piece of soiled cardboard which had been used to plug a hole in the sole of the shoe hung out like a tired dog's tongue. Further down the road the other shoe sat on the road as if it wanted to go somewhere.

His khaki trousers had been ripped at the back and nobody minded his dirty underwear which was soaking with blood. Blood came out of his mouth in a thick trickle and made a dark puddle on the sand. The distended nostrils were choked with more blood. By the slow up and down movement of his humped body people knew he was still alive but was having difficulty in breathing.

Charles Mungoshi

Exercises

Is the author trying to make thc rcader

1 – sympathetic
   – laugh
   – upset
   – annoyed?

Is the author trying to be

2 – cruel
   – amusing
   – unfeeling
   – disgusting?

Is an accident in which a person is injured usually presented

3 – with sympathy
   – without feeling (objectively)
   – lightheartedly?

Is there anything unusual about the way this author relates his story of an accident?

Extract from *Let sleeping vets lie*

I took my leave of Mr Crump with reluctance and as I settled in the seat of the car trying to remember where first gear was situated I could see his bulky form silhouetted against the light from the kitchen; he was waving his hand with gentle benevolence and it struck me as I drove away what a deep and wonderful friendship had been forged that night.

Driving at walking pace along the dark narrow road, my nose almost touching the windscreen, I was conscious of some unusual sensations. My mouth and lips felt abnormally sticky as I though I had been drinking liquid glue instead of wine, my breath seemed to be whistling in my nostrils like a strong wind blowing under a door, and I was having difficulty focusing my eyes. Fortunately I met only one car and as it approached and flashed past in the other direction I was muzzily surprised by the fact that it had two complete sets of headlights which kept merging into each other and drawing apart again.

James Herriot

Exercises

1   What impression is the author trying to create – one that is matter-of-fact or amusing?

2   Can you tell from the very last sentence whether the person telling the story is drunk or sober? Does the tone of the passage differ depending on whether you think the person is drunk or sober?

Section B Language work

Sentence composition

Ambiguous sentences

Take the well-known saying

All that glitters is not gold

The normal meaning of this is that some things that glitter are gold but some things that glitter are not gold. However, taken in a literal, logical, mathematical sense 'All that glitters is not gold' means that whatever glitters is *not* gold. In other words, all glittering things are something else other than gold, which thereby suggests that gold does not glitter.

It is possible to get the two meanings by saying the sentence with two different pronunciations. Read the following aloud and compare the pronunciations (intonations) of the underlined part:

1 <u>We did not do it because we like you.</u> We did it because it was right.

2 <u>We did not do it because we like you.</u> It would not have been good for you.

At the end (i.e. <u>like you</u>) of the underlined part in 1, notice that your voice goes up, whereas at the end of the highlighted part in 2 your voice stays level. This difference in intonation makes it easier for the hearer to understand that in 1 'we did it' whereas in 2 'we did not do it'.

The underlined part is exactly the same in 1 as it is in 2 and there is no written mark to help the reader to understand the meaning. To make 1 clearer you can move 'not' to its 'proper' position, i.e.

We did it, *not* because we like you ...

You should therefore understand:

- That differences in meaning made clear by pronunciation are not represented in writing all the time

- how ambiguity can be created for the reader and can be avoided if it is not necessary

Exercises

1   Say aloud the following sentences in *two* ways to make the meanings clearer for the hearer.

   i   I don't lend my records to anyone.

   ii   All the people were not told.

   iii   We did not tell you because we did not trust you.

   iv   The election did not take place specifically because you couldn't come.

   v   The man didn't die because you performed the operation.

2   Reword each of the previous sentences in *two* ways to make the differences clear for the reader.

Vocabulary

Exercise

Choose the most suitable word from the list to fill in the gaps in these sentences.

1   The new forms will ... owners of small businesses to work out their own accounts.
   aid   help   ease

2   They did all sorts of ... acts to get US dollars out of the country.
   elicit   illicit   illegitimate

3   Not having had a good SBA, he is ... to fail the subject.
   libel   apt   liable

4   He was ... to the proposal from the very beginning.
   averse   adverse   obverse

5   I would ... you not to do whatever you see your friends doing.
   council   consul   counsel

6   Her method of doing things, they had to admit, was most ... in that post.
    effective   efficacious   efficient

7   His later writings, especially his poems, are full of sexual ... .
    illusions   allusions   delusions

8   The principal has ... three good reasons for the improvement in your report.
    sited   cited   sighted

9   For hundreds of years people have been saying that God's coming is ....
    immanent   imminent   eminent

10 They sought to ... Marley's memory by erecting a statue of him in the middle of the city.
    perpatrate   permeate   perpetuate

Punctuation

Linking and introducing

Colon (:)

A colon indicates explicitly that what follows is an explanation, an example or an amplification of what precedes.

   There are many examples of colons throughout this book. Pick them out for yourself.

Dash (–)

The single dash is used to link a phrase or clause which explains, amplifies or finishes a preceding clause. E.g.

> Specialised computer programs can help writers to do what I call flexible composing – a process in which writers compose text as they continue planning.

> They are stimulated to write after doing some programming because they are creating pictures by using words – the words of the programming language.

Hyphen (-)

The hyphen is used to make two (or more words) into one. E.g.

> a good-for-nothing person

> a step-by-step method

It is also used at the end of a line to indicate that a word is unfinished and continues at the beginning of the next line.

Enclosing

Two brackets, two commas and two dashes perform similar functions. The information that is put within two brackets, two commas or two dashes is additional or extra – the rest of the sentence can get along quite well without it. E.g.

> The boys, who were there, were delighted. The girls, who were not, were sad.

> Unfortunately the differences between 'dialect' and standard – whatever pundits agree that is, or whatever it really is locally – are very great sometimes.

Inverted commas are double or single. It does not matter which you use as long as you are consistent. Whatever you are enclosing, whether it is speech or a quotation, you begin with the inverted commas and you end with them. In writing it is very easy to forget to put in the one(s) at the end.

If there is a quotation within a quotation, distinguish between the two by using single marks for one and double for the other. If both end at the same point, separate the one from the other. E.g. ' " or " ' .

Inverted commas may be used for titles, quoted words, highlighted words, foreign words.

Exercise

1   Study the punctuation marks in the following passage and then fill in the blanks with appropriate dialogue:

> '.....?' Mary asked quietly.

> '.....,' replied her sister.

> '..... "....." .....' said Mary, 'and..... "....." .....'

> '.....,' her sister agreed.

2   In each of the following spaces insert a clause which adds to the meaning but does not affect the basic structure of the sentence:

i   Hurricanes ... are disastrous.

ii   I know that cane fires ... spread very rapidly.

iii   Potatoes and yams ... contain fibre.

iv   The committee concluded that alcohol ... caused more deaths than cancer.

v   Please return that video-tape ... before I come home tonight.

Different Kinds of Poetry

This unit will help you to:

✓ understand what makes a poem
✓ know that dramatic, narrative and lyric poems have different characteristics
✓ use some irregular past forms of verbs
✓ understand how prefixes and suffixes influence spelling

Section A
Guidance

Some points to remember about poetry:

- One of the main ingredients of poetry is emotion.

- A poem has meaning – meaning that goes beyond the dictionary and beyond the text.

- Poetic language is condensed – rhythm, rhyme and metre are responsible for the condensed nature of poetic language.

- Poetic language often uses images, symbols and rhetoric.

- The poet has licence to experiment with words, phrases, clauses and grammar in order to achieve his or her purpose.

- Poems are of many types.

Identifying a poem

It is easy in most cases to identify a poem, or, in other words, to distinguish it from an essay or a letter. When it is written, the poem has a format of its own – it normally has lines that do not extend right across the page. You can therefore recognise its written form before you read it.

The length of the line, however, is meant to reflect the sound of the poem and it is the *sound* that distinguishes the poem from other forms of literature. Each line of the poem is supposed to have a certain rhythm and a certain number of beats (which gives it its length). It may also have lines that rhyme at the end. In essence, then, there is no difference between a poem and a song – many songs in their written form are poems. There are, of course, differences that arise from singing on the one hand and reading or reciting on the other. Dub songs are a good example of the way in which a strong beat, rhyme and music can be combined to produce popular and appealing poetry.

In this unit we will look at three different kinds of poetry:

- dramatic poetry
- narrative poetry
- lyric poetry

Dramatic poetry

This is the kind of verse that occurs in a play or is poetry that can be acted out as if it were a play. It is the actual speech of one or more of the characters. Shakespeare's plays, for example, are written in verse and are therefore dramatic (= play) poetry.

Here is an example of a dramatic poem.

If we must die

If we must die, let it not be like hogs
Hunted and penned in an inglorious spot,
While round us bark the mad and hungry dogs,
Making their mock at our accursed lot.
If we must die, O let us nobly die,
So that our precious blood may not be shed
In vain; then even the monsters we defy
Shall be constrained to honour us though dead!
O kinsmen! we must meet the common foe!
Though far outnumbered let us show us brave,
And for their thousand blows deal one deathblow!
What though before us lies the open grave?
Like men we'll face the murderous, cowardly pack,
Pressed to the wall, dying, but fighting back!

Claude McKay

Questions

1 Who do you think is speaking?

2 Who is the person speaking to? (Your answer must identify a specific word in the poem.)

3 What is the situation?

4 Why is the person making the speech?

5 Convert the first four lines of the poem into normal spoken English.

Narrative poetry

This tells a story. Some narrative poems are long, covering one, two or several volumes. Such long narrative poems are called 'epics', and they usually tell the story of the history of a people or country. The most famous and oldest poetry is epic poetry. In West Africa special persons, sometimes called griots, had the job of preserving and telling the history of the tribe in verse. There was no written version of these poems. The epic poems of the ancient Greek and Roman were written down however.

A narrative poem in short stanzas is called a ballad and it usually tells the story of one particular person or incident. Here is an example of a ballad.

Ballad of the landlord

Landlord, landlord,
My roof has sprung a leak.
Don't you 'member I told you about it
Way last week?

Landlord, landlord,
These steps is broken down.
When you come up yourself
It's a wonder you don't fall down.

Ten Bucks you say I owe you?
Ten Bucks you say is due?
Well, that's Ten Bucks more'n I'll pay you
Till you fix this house up new.

What? You gonna get eviction orders?
You gonna cut off my heat?
You gonna take my furniture and
Throw it in the street?

Um-huh! You talking high and mighty.
Talk on – till you get through.
You ain't gonna be able to say a word
If I land my fist on you.

Police! Police!
Come and get this man!
He's trying to ruin the government
And overturn the land!

Copper's whistle!
Patrol bell!
Arrest.
Precinct Station.
Iron cell.
Headlines in press:
MAN THREATENS LANDLORD
TENANT HELD NO BAIL
JUDGE GIVES NEGRO 90 DAYS IN COUNTY JAIL

Langston Hughes

Questions

1 Who is telling the story in the first five stanzas?

2 Who is telling the story in the next stanza?

3 Who is telling the story in the last part?

4 Are the words in the first five stanzas serious or amusing or both? Say why you think so.

5 In the next stanza is the person afraid or annoyed? Explain your answer.

6 Why does the poet use dialect in the first five stanzas?

Lyric poetry

This style of poem is fairly short and expresses emotion. Most poetry falls into this category. There are many types of lyric poetry, but the most common are:

- *sonnets*, which usually deal with love

- *elegies*, which usually deal with death

- *odes*, which set out to offer praise

- *limericks*, which are meant to be humorous

Here is an example of a lyric poem.

Sympathy

I know what the caged bird feels, alas!
When the sun is bright on the <u>upland slopes</u>;
When the wind stirs soft through the springing grass,
And the river flows like a <u>stream of glass</u>;
When the first bird sings and the first bud opes,
And the faint perfume from its <u>chalice</u> steals –
I know what the caged bird feels!

I know why the caged bird beats his wing
Till its blood is red on the cruel bars
For he must fly back to his perch and cling
When <u>he fain would be</u> on the bough <u>a-swing</u>;
And a pain still throbs in the old, old scars
And they pulse again with a <u>keener sting</u> –
I know why he beats his wing!
I know why the caged bird sings, ah me,
When his wing is bruised and his bosom sore, –
When he beats his bars and he would be free;
It is not a carol of joy or glee,
But a prayer that he sends from <u>his heart's deep core,</u>
But a plea, that upward to Heaven he flings –
I know why the caged bird sings!

Paul Laurence Dunbar

Questions

1 Why is the poem called *Sympathy*?

2 According to the poet, why does the caged bird sing?

3 List all the painful things which make you feel sorry for the bird.

4 Explain the meaning of the underlined words.

5 Write a short letter to a friend explaining why your pet canary is happy to be in its cage.

Assignment

In whatever poetry anthologies you have available find examples of these three kinds of poetry. Choose poems which you particularly like, and be prepared to read them out in class.

Section B Language work

Sentence composition

Irregular/Unusual past forms of verbs in English

Some English verbs do not behave as you would expect when put into the past form. E.g.

1 'born' is used with 'be'; 'borne' is used with 'have'.

I was born ten years ago.

She has borne two children. (not 'borned')

2 'hanged' is used with persons; 'hung' is used with things.

They hanged him.

They hung it up.

Exercise

Say which of the two words in brackets is the correct one in the following sentences:

1 The thief (robbed/stole) his money.

2 The workers have (laid/lain) the boxes on the ground.

3 The dog was (lying/laying) dead in the road.

4 The boat has (sunk/sank).

5 The boat (sunk/sank) last year.

6 Today the water has (raised/risen) another inch in the tank.

7 The body was (laid/lain) to rest.

8 The old lady has (laid/lain) down to sleep.

Spelling

Prefixes and suffixes

A prefix is the part of a word which comes at the beginning. E.g.

> en̲sure, re̲place, un̲do, im̲plant.

A suffix is the part of a word which comes at the end. E.g.

> want̲ed, sing̲ing, eat̲s̲, prepar̲ation.

Suffixes which sound the same

Suffixes that have the same sound pose problems for spelling. For example the suffixes '-ents' and '-ence' sound the same, but some people do not know when to use the one or the other.

Consider the following words:

incidents	incidence
independents	independence
patients	patience
presents	presence
correspondents	correspondence
precedents	precedence
residents	residence

'-ents' is the plural of '-ent'. It mostly refers to things which you can count/identify one by one. In other words, you can say ' five incidents, independents, patients,' etc.

'-ence' is not a plural ending and it usually (not always) refers to something abstract. You cannot use numbers with '-ence', e.g. you cannot say 'five residence, incidence, presence', etc.

(*Note*: There is the same difference between '-ants' and '-ance'. E.g. assistants assistance.)

Confusing prefixes

For some related words it is difficult to remember their different prefixes. The following six pairs of words are examples of this confusion:

accept	except	elicit	illicit
affect	effect	emigrant	immigrant
allusion	illusion	eminent	imminent

Accurate pronunciation

Pronouncing words carefully can help you to spell and work out the meaning of some words. A distinction which gives some people trouble is the one between:

'co-operate' and 'corporate'

In this case, if you remember that the 'co-' in 'co-operate' is a prefix, you will find the word easier to pronounce and you will not be tempted to write 'incooperate'. On the other hand, if you remember corporate as one word, the spelling and pronunciation of it and also of incorporated (abbreviated as Inc.) should be easier.

The suffix '-able'

Note the spelling of the following three words when you add the suffix '-able':

noticeable   changeable   manageable

Note that some words have more than one correct spelling:

judgement   judgment

Exercises

A   A science student, after taking notes in a lecture, wrote the following sentences as answers to questions in a test. Read the sentences carefully and then correct all the spelling mistakes.

1   The differents in rate has to do with the molecules and there absorbtion rate allong with there size.

2   Anticonvulsant activity of barbiturates is inferred by the presents of the phenyl group.

3   The presents of cyclic, branch or unsaturated constituents at position 5 would affect it's lipid solubility.

B   In the passage opposite fill in the blanks by either:

1   inserting a whole word that is suitable and makes sense

2   adding a prefix to the word given

3   adding a suffix to the word given

4   adding both a prefix and a suffix to the word given

(*Note*: Three dots do not mean that three letters are missing.)

The New World was attractive to all ... of persons for different reasons – for some it was money, for others it was adventure, for others ... curiosity about ... and fauna. The view that the ... of the people who came were bank... and criminals ... is based on scanty eviden... and prejudice. It was also misleading when you think that England at that time had a great number of poor and ...literate peasants for whom daily existen... was work from morning ... night. ... such conditions, escape to a new ... was preferable ... many. The inciden... of ...nutrition and child labour promised a tough and short life for the residen... of many counties in England. Many refused to ...cept such a life and, having ... ...fected by the ...lusions of great wealth in the New World, soon became ...migran... to the islands. Naturally, the wealthy landowners who ... home resented this exodus and challenge to their traditional lifestyle and began to paint a ... of savage, crude and ...solute life in the colonies. Such views did not ...crease the attraction of the colonies, but they served to popular... and cement the concept of the sophisticated Englishman and the ...cultured West Indian.

West Indian Poetry

Objectives

This unit will help you to:

- ✓ appreciate the special place of poetry in West Indian society
- ✓ be aware that newspaper poetry, dialect poetry, dub poetry are all forms of West Indian poetry
- ✓ use verbs meaning 'be' or 'become' correctly
- ✓ understand the special spelling problems posed by eye-dialect

Section A Guidance

In the West Indies certain types of poetry have a special place in society. The poets in each case were or are popular poets, expressing themselves in the language of the people and dealing with current or familiar topics.

Newspaper poetry

For a long time, West Indian newspapers have featured characters speaking on topical issues using a local dialect. These may take the form of cartoons, that is, stylised drawings of people with words, or letters from a well-known character to a friend.

In Guyana in the late nineteenth century and in Barbados in the early twentieth century local topical issues were discussed in poetic form in the newspapers. These poetry columns were extremely popular so much so that people bought the newspaper simply to read 'Quow' or 'Lizzie and Joe'.

Poetry was used then for the same reason that cartoons are used today. Since the newspaper is normally written in Standard English, the use of non-standard dialect has to be separated and made special in some way. Dialect poetry allowed the writer to use the speech of the people but at the same time to show his skill as a writer of rhyming verse.

Here is an example of newspaper poetry.

De wishes uh de people Joe

De wishes uh de people Joe
De masses you en me
We voice got much less weight den ef
Dis was crung colony.

But yet Buhbados boasting still
Bout she self-government
Jus read de Guvnah message Joe
Den you will see um ent.

De masses sweat en brawn is wah
Does mek de treasury fat
Why flout duh wishes den en treat dum
Like uh ole black hat?

E. Cordle

Questions

1 Change the words in the verses above into normally spelled English words with correct grammar. Where necessary substitute new words.

2 Why does the author use dialect and what effect does it have?

3 Identify the points or arguments which the speaker is presenting.

Dialect poetry

The two most famous dialect poets in the West Indies are Louise Bennett, who started her work in the late 1930s and Paul Keene-Douglas, who started his in the 1970s. In both cases the poetry is oral and read aloud by the author. The nature and form of Louise Bennett's poems are not very different from the newspaper poetry mentioned above, although Bennett could claim to be a better poet. The great popularity of the poetry results from the fact that it deals with topics that everyone can understand, in language that is appealing, and it is humorous and entertaining. Since the most appealing part of the poetry is the language itself, that is, the sounds, words, expressions of local speech, it is not always understood and appreciated outside its local audience. So, although Louise Bennett is known and loved by Jamaicans far and wide, in the rest of the Caribbean her poetry is not easily understood and does not have the same appeal. Samples from the two poets follow.

Bans o'killing

So yuh a de man, me hear bout!
Ah yuh dem sey dah-teck
Whole heap o' English oat sey dat
Yuh gwine kill dialect!

Meck me get it straight Mass Charlie
For me noh quite undastan,
Yuh gwine kill all English dialect
Or jus Jamaica one?

Ef yuh dah-equal up wid English
Language, den wha meck
Yuh gwine go feel inferior, wen
It come to dialect?

Ef yuh kean sing 'Linstead Market'
An 'Wata come a me y'eye',
Yuh wi haffi tap sing 'Auld lang syne'
An 'Comin thru de rye'.

Dah language weh yuh proud o',
Weh yuh honour and respeck,
Po' Mass Charlie! Yuh noh know sey
Dat it spring from dialect!

Dat dem start fe tun language,
From de fourteen century,
Five hundred years gawn an dem got
More dialect dan we!

Yuh wi haffe kill de Lancashire
De Yorkshire, de Cockney
De broad Scotch an de Irish brogue
Before yuh start kill me!

Yuh wi haffe get de Oxford book
O' English verse, an tear
Out Chaucer, Burns, Lady Grizelle
An plenty o' Shakespeare!

Wen yuh done kill 'wit' an 'humour'
Wen yuh kill 'Variety'
Yuh wi haffe fine a way fe kill
Originality!

An mine how yuh dah-read dem English
Book deh pon yuh shelf
For ef yuh drop a 'h' yuh mighta
Haffe kill yuhself.

Louise Bennett

Questions

1   Try to read the poem aloud so that it makes sense to you and to those listening to you.

2   Underline those words which you do not understand. Say exactly why you do not understand them.

3   The author says that the English language has more dialect in its history than Jamaican dialect itself. What examples of dialect in the English language does the author give?

Exercise

Rewrite the poem (as a poem) in Standard English.

Ole times

Ah want to tell the world 'bout we
In fact 'bout all de boys an' dem,
'bout liming by de lampost – beating pan
Busting ole talk an watching woman.
How we used to pappyshow police
An play respectable when we see priest.
Boy dat concrete eh used to play hard
Pants bottom used to grate way real bad.
An dem spitting competition – man dat was it
Racing lead pencil in drain – penny profit.
You used to be de best sweetman in town
Never mind we mamaguy you – tambrand hound.
'member how we used to peep shango?
Maco wabine and tief mango?
How 'bout drinking rum without chaser,
An crashing wedding – don't talk 'bout theater.
Going to college – boy dat was big ting,
You eh learn much – improve your skeffing.
Dem starch drill pants used to cut me leg
We used to mop snowball but never beg.
De tings we used to do – ah could write a book
But you won't buy – just tief a look.
So these thoughts I leave to you as man,
Long time story – nothing better than.

Paul Douglas

Questions

1   List all the things which the poet used to do as a youngster.

2   List some of the things which you yourself do now which you will talk about when you are old.

3   Identify in the poem words and phrases which are not found in an English dictionary.

4   With the help of an adult explain as many of them as you can.

Dub poetry

In a sense dub poetry is one of the oldest forms of poetry. In the days of the ancient Greeks the poet played a lyre while he was reciting his poetry. Today the dub poet is accompanied by drums or a whole band in a way that heightens the rhythm and beat of the poem. Dub poetry was developed by Jamaicans at home and abroad. So, even where it has spread to non-Jamaican contexts, it still has Jamaican influence in its language. Unlike the dialect poetry of Bennett and Douglas, dub poetry does not provoke a lot of laughter. It deals with serious topics like social problems and injustice in a 'talking song' manner, which does not allow for the kind of audience reaction you would normally get at the end of particularly amusing lines in dialect poetry. Well-known figures like Linton Kwesi Johnson and Mutabaruka are poets who use a musical accompaniment and are not 'singers' who talk. Here is an extract of dub poetry.

Free up de lan'

Free up de lan', white man
free de Namibian
Free up de lan', white man
free all African
Free de black in Englan'
free de Caribbean
Free all nationgs

Mutabaruka

Questions

1   Look up the word dub in a good dictionary and say which of its meanings is related to the meaning in dub poetry.

2   Give your own meaning of the word dub.

3   What makes dub poetry and songs appealing to young people? What makes it annoying to many adults?

4   What is the difference between dub poetry and other poetry?

Songs

Writers of calypsos and reggae songs are very much like dialect poets, except that over the years the words and verses of calypsos have been much closer to Standard English than most people think. Most calypsos are ballads. The calypso is the oldest song-form that is regarded as West Indian. While calypsos are meant to be enjoyed as popular songs, today they have, in many cases, become very sophisticated in their words. The verses of the calypso can therefore be studied and appreciated as poems.

Assignments   **A**   Pair up with another student. Together collect as many examples of newspaper poetry, dialect poetry and dub poetry as you can.

B   Write a poem yourself. Use dialect or Standard English. Decide on the kind of poem you want to write, looking back to Unit 9 if necessary. For the content, think about something you feel strongly about – your feelings will help you write the poem. Keep it short.

**Section B
Language
work**

Sentence composition

'Be' and 'become'

A number of verbs which can mean 'be' or 'become' are followed by adjectives and not adverbs.

Become	*Be*
grew strong	smell sweet
turn sour	look good
fall ill	look well (adjective = 'in good health')
run wild	taste great
go bad	feel unwell
wear thin	seem strange
come right	appear foolish
	sound strange, cracked

Note that 'well' can be either an adjective or an adverb. Note also that a number of words ending in 'ly' are adjectives and not adverbs. E.g.

silly, sickly, mannerly, manly, gentlemanly

a silly idea

a sickly child

a mannerly boy

a manly deed

the gentlemanly thing to do

In informal speech in the West Indies the meanings 'be' and 'become' are often rendered in a way that is different from International English.

Note the following [W.I. = West Indian English; I.E. = International English]:

W.I. It making hot. (the weather)
I.E. It is hot.

W.I. The forest was making dark.
I.E. The forest was dark.

W.I. It smells stink.
I.E. It stinks. / It is stinking.

Spelling

Eye-dialect

This is the alteration of normal spelling to give a visual picture of what a specific dialect sounds like. Normal spelling is altered by adding or leaving out letters and by using the apostrophe. Examples are *fo'*, *'pon*, *lickle* (little), *befo'* (before).

One problem with eye-dialect is that it does not and cannot give, in spite of strong belief to the contrary, an accurate representation of the sounds of actual speech. This is because each letter of the alphabet represents more than one sound: the author may intend one sound whereas the reader interprets another.

A further problem is that, because the reader has to pause to decipher every word written in eye-dialect, the flow and intonation which speech has is lost unless the reader reads the passage over more than once.

For this reason some West Indian authors do not alter normal English spelling very much, but prefer to concentrate on West Indian sentence structure (order of words, adding words, leaving out words) rather than on West Indian pronunciation.

Eye-dialect is popular with newspaper columnists and cartoonists where the local reader has a better chance of interpreting the pronunciation the author intends. In short stories written for a wider audience it is better to concentrate on the words, expressions, idioms and sentence structure of the characters when they speak, with occasional eye-dialect, rather than to concentrate consistently on pronunciation.

Exercises

Collect from a newspaper, magazine or book five examples of cartoons depicting local characters and their speech. Look at the words and:

1 say which words you would spell differently

2 rewrite the cartoon with a Standard English version

3 select one of the cartoons and expand it into a short story of about 100 words

The Meaning of Poetry

Objectives

This unit will help you to:

✓ understand how double meanings, figurative language (simile, metaphor, personification) and allusions are used in poetry
✓ work out the meaning of poems
✓ practise some difficult noun/verb agreements
✓ think about the meaning of some idioms
✓ appreciate the spelling rules about doubling letters

Section A Guidance

Poetry has a tight structure, i.e. everything has to fit into lines of a certain length and stanzas of a certain length. There is therefore not a great deal of explanation, which means that the reader has to make a greater effort to understand.

Other factors which make poetry more difficult to understand are:

- double meaning

- figurative language

- allusions

- context

- changes in meanings over the years

Double meaning

Double meaning is such a normal part of calypsos that the listeners are accustomed to looking for underlying meanings. Consider the following lines from a well-known old calypso.

Bendwood Dick

Tell your sister to come down here
I got something for she
Tell she it's Mr Bendwood Dick
The man from Sangre Grande

She know me well
I had she already
Go on, go on!
Tell she Mr Bendwood come

The Mighty Sparrow

Questions

1   Why do the words 'something', 'know', 'had' allow the listener to add a more 'exciting' meaning to the lines?

2   Do you always look for 'other' meanings? Why do you?

3   Do such suggestive words appeal to men only? Would you ban or discourage songs with such words? Give reasons for your answers.

4   Is the meaning in the word itself or does the 'mind' of the hearer put in the 'other' meaning?

5   What does the word salacious mean?

6   Many popular singers throughout the West Indies are noted for the clever way that they play with words. In addition, many people claim that a calypsonian who uses plainly vulgar and obscene words would not be appreciated. Do you think this is true?

7   Compose a song (ballad, calypso, reggae or other) for a class competition.

Figurative language

Poetry, because it is emotional, tries to produce sharp and strong sensations or pictures. This the poet tries to do by taking the literal language with its everyday meanings and twisting it around, putting a word with another one that it does not usually go with or by giving things characteristics that they do not normally have.

Three terms which are used to capture the ways in which the poet uses the language are:

- simile
- metaphor
- personification

Similes

The simile is a comparison of one thing with another in which the word 'as' or 'like' is used.

Time, like a never ending stream,
Bears all its sons away.
They fly, forgotten as a dream
Dies at the opening day.

Isaac Watts

There are two similes in the previous verse. Firstly, time is compared to a stream which goes on and on. Secondly, the poet (song-writer) says that people die and are forgotten in the same way that a dream dies and is forgotten at daybreak. The comparison of life with dreaming is very common in literature.

Metaphors

The metaphor is a comparison which does not use the words 'as' and 'like' and in fact makes it seem as if one thing is another.

I can hear the gospel
Of little feet
Go choiring
Down the dusty asphalt street.

Roger Mais

Here the poet is describing children going home from school, and he uses the words 'gospel' and 'choiring' as metaphors for the noise being made by the children's feet. He uses the word 'gospel' to compare the sound of the children's feet to 'glad tidings'; and the word 'choiring' to compare the noise with the many voices in a choir. Because of his choice of metaphors we can tell that the author therefore has a pleasant reaction to the noise of the children.

Personification

Personification is a specific kind of metaphor which gives human qualities to things which in reality do not have such qualities. Note the following:

I saw day creep across the sky
And dawn slip slowly by
And the grey sun put on its dress
Of blue midsummer loveliness
I heard the wind rustle in the tree
And in a whisper seem to say
'The night has gone, it is now the day.'

Sheryl Gordon

In addition to personification poets often treat inanimate things as if they have animal qualities.

Allusion

While some poetry deals with eternal subjects like love and happiness, other poetry deals with specific historical incidents, not in a straightforward narration of events, but through a series of allusions to events. You need to know something about those events in order to appreciate the poem.

In the calypso *Haiti* David Rudder alludes to a number of events. Once these are pointed out to you, you will find the poem easy to understand.

Haiti

Toussaint was a mighty man
And to make matters worse he was black.
Black back in the days when black men knew
Their place was in the back.
But this rebel he walked through Napoleon   5
Who thought that wasn't very nice.
And so today my brothers in Haiti
They still pay the price.

Chorus
Haiti, I'm sorry
We've misunderstood you.   10
One day we'll turn our heads
And look inside you.
Haiti, I'm sorry
Haiti, I'm sorry
One day we'll turn our heads   15
Restore your glory.

Many hands reached out to St Georges
And are still reaching out
And to those frightened,
Foolish men of Pretoria   20
We still scream and shout
We came together in song
To steady the horn of Africa
But the papaloa come and the babyloa go
And still we don't seem to care.   25

When there is anguish in Port-au-Prince
Don't you know it's still Africa crying?
We are outing fires in far away places
When our neighbours are burning
The middle passage is gone   30
So how come
Overcrowded boats still haunt our lives?
I refuse to believe that we good people
Will forever turn our hearts
And our eyes away.   35

David Michael Rudder

Explanatory notes on the text

Line 1:   Pierre Dominique Toussaint-Breda(1743–1803), nicknamed 'L'Ouverture', a slave until he was about 50, became leader in the slave revolt in Haiti and in 1799 became the first black ruler of Haiti.

Line 2:   In the New World in those days it was unthinkable for a black man to be a leader of a country.

Lines 3–4:   Whites were given preference of place in all matters. Note, for example, that Martin Luther King's rise to fame started when he championed the cause of a black woman who refused to sit in the back of the bus in one of the southern states in the USA. Note also the once well-known saying 'If you white, you alright; if you black, stand back'.

Line 5:   Not strictly true. Napoleon imprisoned Toussaint; it was Dessalines who defeated Napoleon's army and proclaimed Haiti independent in 1804.

Lines 6–8:   Haiti ostracised since then because of white racism.

Line 10:   West Indians know little of Haiti.

Line 15:   The oldest Negro republic and the second oldest free nation in the Western Hemisphere.

Line 17:   American Intervention in Grenada (Toussaint was born in Grenada).

Line 18:   Reach out = to give aid.

Line 21:   Constant condemnation of apartheid in South Africa.

Lines 22–23: The song 'We are the world', released to help the people of Ethiopia during the famine of 1984–5.

Line 24:   Papa Doc and Baby Doc Duvalier; 'loa' is the Haitian word for 'spirit' or 'god'.

Line 28:   African diaspora.

Assignment   Write a poem about one main incident. In the poem do the following:

- use some dialect

- include at least two metaphors

Section B Language work	**Sentence composition**

Sentence composition

Difficult noun/verb agreement

Most nouns in English are quite straightforward in the way that they form their plurals. E.g.

> cat/cats   fly/flies

There are some words which have plurals which look a little unusual but after a time you get accustomed to them. E.g.

> datum/data   radius/radii

However, there are a number of nouns in English which are much more troublesome and it is not always easy to remember whether the verb they go with should be singular or plural and whether the pronoun which replaces them should be 'it' or 'they'.

1 *Nouns whose singular form is the same as their plural.* E.g.

> sheep, salmon, Chinese, Japanese, means, series, species, *dice,
>
> *innings

(*Note*: * The word 'die' is the singular of 'dice', but it is regarded as old-fashioned, except by Americans.
* Americans use 'inning' for singular and 'innings' for plural.)

Examples

> A means of stopping holes is by using lint.
>
> There are several means of stopping holes.
>
> One innings is forty overs.
>
> The two innings are a total of eighty overs.
>
> A Japanese is an Asian.
>
> Chinese tend to be short in comparison with other races.

2 *Nouns which can be singular or plural depending on what they mean.* E.g.

> statistics, acoustics

Examples

> Statistics is a course, but statistics are facts and figures.
>
> Acoustics is the study of sound, but acoustics are the qualities of sounds that you hear.

3 *Nouns which have no singular form.* E.g.

>   amends, banns, greens, outskirts, remains, thanks, surroundings

Examples

>   Amends were made.
>
>   Banns were published.
>
>   Greens are good for you.
>
>   The outskirts come into sight when you reach the top.
>
>   His mortal remains were solemnly interred.
>
>   Thanks are in order.
>
>   The surroundings were not clean.

4 *Nouns which can be used with 'a pair of' and are plural when used* without *'a pair of'*. E.g.

>   pyjamas, binoculars, pliers, trousers, pants, jeans, scissors, tights

Examples

>   My pyjamas are on the line.
>
>   I cannot see through those binoculars.
>
>   These pliers are no good; I need a good pair.
>
>   His jeans have a stain on the left leg and the seat.
>
>   The scissors were kept on the open Bible.
>
>   I am not wearing these tights. They got caught on a nail.

(*Note*: Even though it seems as if you are dealing with a single item, i.e. one garment or one instrument, the word itself [pyjamas, pliers, etc.] is plural. You therefore have to use a plural verb following and a plural pronoun to replace it.)

5 *The word 'police' gives some people trouble.* The word is followed by a plural verb and replaced by the pronoun 'they'.

Examples

>   The police are the guardians of the society.
>
>   When you call the police, they usually respond.

If you want to talk about one or more members of the police force, use policeman or policewoman. Do not use police to refer to individual members of the force. For instance, do not say 'He is a bad police' or 'I saw two police riding horses'.

Vocabulary

Idioms

An idiom is an expression peculiar to a language, which cannot be logically or grammatically explained.

Exercise

Explain the meaning of the following idioms.

1   To blow your own trumpet

2   To paddle your own canoe

3   To give oneself airs

4   To put your best foot forward

5   To sell oneself to the highest bidder

6   To sell oneself short

7   To sell oneself

Spelling

Doubling letters

Knowing when to double a letter in a word can be difficult. You need to double the consonant:

- if the word ends with a consonant

- if you are adding an ending beginning with a vowel

- if the last syllable of the word is stressed *OR* the word has one syllable.

Examples

occur: occurring, occurred

trap: trapping, trapped

fit: fitting, fitted

stop: stopping, stopped

admit: admitting, admitted

refer: referring, referred

But note that these words also double the last consonant:

kidnap, counsel, label, handicap

Do not double the consonant if the first syllable of the word is stressed.

E.g.   cater/catering   water/watering

But note that these words *do* double the last consonant:

worship, travel, signal, quarrel

Exercise

Fill in the blanks below.

step	....	....
....	expelling	....
....	writing	....
fulfil	....	....
....	staring	....
occur	....	....
....	....	harassed
....	quarrelling	....
control	....	....
....	....	embarrassed
....	....	stressed
plane	....	....
....	filling	....
....	....	fitted
....	....	developed
....	hitting	....
quit	....	....
....	falling	....
....	....	distilled
....	telling	....
....	wedding	....
....	....	hopped
....	recalling	....
spell	....	....

Understanding the Context of Poetry

Objectives

This unit will help you to:

- ✓ appreciate how poems have different contexts
- ✓ understand the particular problems of dealing with older texts
- ✓ learn how the repetition of sounds in poetry creates special effects
- ✓ practise converting sentences into Standard English
- ✓ expand your vocabulary: the language of poetry

Section A Guidance

An appreciation of the world the poet wants to create, the context for the poem, is necessary for a fuller understanding of any poetry.

Romantic context

Many poets over the years have painted pictures of Nature – they have described rivers, oceans, forests, fields, flowers, expressing their feelings about these elements of Nature. In most of these 'Romantic' poems the flow of language and the colourfulness of the adjectives, verbs and nouns create the scenery or context within which the poet expresses or suggests his real theme. In the following poem there is an interweaving of themes: the slave's previous freedom is set against the context of the natural beauty of West Africa; it is then contrasted with his present bondage.

The slave's dream

Beside the ungathered rice he lay, his sickle in his hand;
His breast was bare, his <u>matted</u> hair was buried in the sand.
Again, in the mist and shadow of sleep, he saw his native land.

Wide through the landscape of his dreams the lordly Niger flowed;
Beneath the palm-trees on the plain once more a king he strode,
And heard the tinkling caravans descend the mountain-road.

He saw once more his dark-eyed queen among her children stand;
They clasped his neck, they kissed his cheeks, they held him by the hand! –
A tear burst from the sleeper's lids, and fell into the sand.

And then at furious speed he rode along the Niger's bank; His bridle-
  reins were golden chains, and, with a martial clank,
At each leap he could feel his <u>scabbard</u> of steel smiting his stallion's flank.

Before him, like a blood-red flag, the bright flamingos flew;
From morn till night he followed their flight, o'er plains where the
  tamarind grew,
Till he saw the roofs of <u>Caffre</u> huts, and the ocean rose to view.

At night he heard the lion roar, and the hyena scream,
And the river-horse, as he crushed the reeds beside some hidden
  stream
And it passed, <u>like a glorious roll of drums</u>, through the triumph of his
  dream.

The forest, <u>with their myriad tongues,</u> shouted of liberty;
And the blast of the desert cried aloud, with a voice so wild and free,
That he started in his sleep and smiled at their <u>tempestuous</u> glee.

He did not feel the driver's whip, nor the burning heat of day,
For death had <u>illumined</u> the land of sleep, and his lifeless body lay
A worn-out <u>fetter</u> that the soul had broken and thrown away.

H.W. Longfellow

Questions

1 Pick out the words and phrases in the previous poem which you regard as 'poetic'.

2 Where is the slave, what is he doing there and what had he been doing?

3 Where is the Niger and what is the slave's dream about?

4 Describe in one paragraph, using your own words as much as possible, the lifestyle of the slave before he became a slave.

5 The second last stanza contains examples of personification. What does the forest symbolise and why?

6 Explain the meaning of the words and phrases underlined as they are used in the poem.

7 Why is context important in this poem?

Realistic context

In the following poem by Michael Smith the context is a market scene with a Rasta in the midst of it. Whereas the poet in the previous poem was 'romantic', the poet here is realistic and this is reflected in his language. For he not only gives the impression of hustle and bustle and many people talking and confrontation, but the language is that of the people, including that of the Rasta. The regular rhythm and nature of the previous poem are not a part of this poem. A market scene gives the impression of confusion and contrast so there are lines of different lengths, repetitions, statements, exclamations, questions, threats, quotations, sung parts, all of which help create the atmosphere of a market-place.

I an I alone or Goliath

I an I alone
ah trod tru creation
Babylon on I right
Babylon on I left
Babylon in front of I
an Babylon behine I
an I an I alone inna de middle
like a Goliath wid a sling shot

'Ten cent a bundle fi me calaloo!
Yuh a buy calaloo, dread? Ten cent.'

Everybody a try fi sell something
Everybody a try fi grab something
Everybody a try fi hussle something
Everybody a try fi kill something

but ting an ting mus ring
an only a few cyaan sing
cause dem nah face de same sinting

'It's a hard road to travel
 and a mighty long way to go;
 Jesus; me blessed Saviour
 will meet us on the journey home.' (*Sung*)

'Shoppin bag! Shoppin bag! Five cent fi one!' 'Green pepper!
Thyme! Skellion! Pimento!'
'Remember de Sabbath day to keep it holy!
Six days shalt thou labour,
but on the seventh day shalt thou rest.'
'Hey, Mam! How much fi dah piece a yam deh?
No, no dat; dat! Yes, dat!'
'Three dollars a poun, nice genkleman.'
'Clear out! Oonoo country people
too damn tief!' 'Like yuh muma!'
'Fi-me muma? Wha yuh know bout me muma?'
'Look-ya, a might push dis inna yuh!'
'Yuh lie! A woulda collar yuh!'
'Bruck it up! But dread, cool down!'
'Alright, cool down, Rastafari.'

Michael Smith

Questions

1   Do you think the poet is talking about something more than a market scene? Justify your answer.

2   Suppose someone said 'I an I alone' is not poetry, how would you defend Michael Smith, or, on the other hand, why would you agree with the person?

3   Why does the poet use Standard English spelling sometimes and eye-dialect at other times?

4   Which phrases are examples of Rasta speech?

Understanding older texts

Many of the hymns which are sung in churches are written in older English, which is not as easy to understand as it may at first seem. For example, take these first two lines of the famous Christian hymn

> There is a green hill far away
> Without a city wall.

To understand these lines it is vital for you to know that in older English 'without' meant the opposite to 'within'. The lines are saying that the hill was outside the city wall.

Many older poems have words which are not often used today, but which it is important to understand. Remember that many West Indians are fond of the Bible, which contains in its older versions words with older meanings.

In order to understand older texts you need to know something about the context (the ways, habits, items, jobs, hobbies, clothes, etc.) which were normal at the time that the author was writing. This background knowledge has to be gained from many different sources e.g. history, geography, social studies.

Sometimes words and phrases appear in a different order in older poems. It is the sentence structure of older texts which presents the greatest difficulty to the modern reader. Let us now look at two poems, noting the meanings of words which have changed over time or which are unusual, noting also the order of the words and clauses.

A psalm of life

Tell me not, in mournful *numbers,   * poetry
Life is but an empty dream!
For the soul is dead that slumbers,
And things are not what they seem.

Life is real! life is *earnest!   * serious
And the grave is not its goal;
'Dust thou art, to dust returnest,'
Was not spoken of the soul.

Not enjoyment, and not sorrow,
Is our destined end or way
But to act that each to-morrow
Find us further than to-day.

Art is long, and Time is fleeting,
And our hearts, though *stout and brave,   * strong
Still, like muffled drums, are beating
Funeral marches to the grave.

In the world's broad field of battle,
In the *bivouac of life,   * campaign
Be not like dumb, driven cattle!
Be a hero in the strife!

Trust no Future, howe'er pleasant!
Let the dead Past bury its dead!
Act – act in the living Present!
Heart within, and God o'erhead!

Lives of great men all remind us
We can make our lives *sublime;   * noble
And, *departing, leave behind us   * dying
Footprints on the sands of time,

Footprints that perhaps another,
Sailing o'er life's solemn main,
A *forlorn and shipwrecked brother,   * lonely
Seeing, shall take heart again.

Let us, then, be up and doing,
With a heart for any fate;
Still achieving, still pursuing,
Learn to labour and to wait.

H. W. Longfellow

Questions   1   Why is the poem called *A psalm of life*?

2   What is the poet advising us to do?

3   Do you agree with the philosophy which the poet is advocating in the
very last line of the poem?

Casabianca (The boy stood on the burning deck)

The boy stood on the burning deck,
Whence all but* he had fled;   *from which everybody
The flame, that lit the battle's wreck,   except
Shone round him – o'er the dead.
Yet beautiful and bright he stood,
As* born to rule the storm;   *as if
A creature of heroic blood,
A proud though child-like form!

The flames rolled on – he would not go,
Without his father's word*; –   *orders
That father, faint* in death below*,   *lifeless   *below deck
His voice no longer heard.
He called aloud: 'Say, father! say
If yet my task is done?' –
He knew not that the chieftain lay
Unconscious of his son.

'Speak, father!' once again he cried,
'If I may yet be gone!
And' – but the booming shots replied,
And fast the flames rolled on.
Upon his brow he felt their breath,
And in his waving hair,
And looked from that lone post of death,
In still, yet brave despair;
And shouted but once more aloud,
'My father! must I stay?'
While o'er him fast, through sail and shroud*,   *ropes
The wreathing fires made way: from the mast
They wrapped the ship in splendour wild,
They caught the flag on high,
And streamed above the gallant child,
Like banners in the sky.

There came a burst of thunder sound, –
The boy! – oh, where was he?
Ask of the winds, that far around
With fragments strewed* the sea,–   *scattered over
With mast, and helm, and pennon fair*,   *flag unblemished
That well had borne their part*!   *performed well
But the noblest thing that perished there,
Was that young faithful heart!

Mrs Hemans

Questions   1 Would you say that the boy in the poem was heroic or stupid? Why?

2 Which of the following does the poem deal with: heroism; obedience; sacrifice; war; love; sailing?

Assignment   Look in a hymn book for hymns which use words in an unusual way. Try to find three or four examples for discussion in class.

Section B Language work

Language: Repetition of sounds in poetry

When you are reading poetry, the length of the lines will cause you to 'pronounce' (recite) the words in a certain way. The 'music' of poetry is based on the pitch, stress and length of the vowels. Just as there is repetition in the beat in a poem, there is also deliberate repetition in the word-sounds. This can be done through:

- rhyme – recurrence of a sound at the end of lines

- alliteration – recurrence of a sound at the beginning of words

- consonance – the recurrence of a sound at various places

The following is an example of alliteration:

> Dismissed <u>w</u>ith sneers he packed his tools and <u>w</u>ent,
> And <u>w</u>andered <u>w</u>orkless; for it seemed un<u>w</u>ise
> to close <u>w</u>ith one who dared to criticise
> And carp on points of taste
> Rude men should <u>w</u>ork <u>w</u>here placed, and be content.

The following is an example of consonance:

> not a sarradee come you cahn fine she <u>in</u> there after leven o'clock
> heat ris<u>in</u>: smok<u>in</u> his<u>in</u> outside: blackbirds hid<u>in</u> from sun white:
> weigh<u>in</u> out flour, chopp<u>in</u> up salt beef,
> count<u>in</u> out biscuit
> shovell<u>in</u>
> oat flake out o de <u>tin</u> while she
> frett<u>in</u>

E. Braithwaite

Sentence composition

Exercise   Convert the following ten sentences into Standard English.

1 They too like to push up themselves.

2 He is always unfairing people.

115

3   He was brakesing going down the hill.

4   The water threw away on her.

5   Throw the ball give me before I come and kick you down.

6   I know you told me must not go, but I don't care.

7   The bus could not pass there, being that it was so narrow.

8   The bank's headquarters is building now.

9   Although I told him not to, he still went and troubled the camera.

10   How far have you got with the house? The roof is putting on now.

Vocabulary

Expanding your vocabulary

These are all words which can be used when talking about poetry. Look at the meanings carefully.

Alliteration:	repetition of the same first sound at the beginning of words
Blank verse:	poetry without rhymes
Limerick:	a humorous poem of five lines
Monologue:	a long speech by one person in a group
Sonnet:	a fourteen-line poem
Griot:	a traditional roving poet, musician and story-teller of West Africa
Literature:	the writings of a nation, era; cultural expression in language
Dramatist:	a writer of plays
Critic:	a judge in literature and art
Critique:	the written opinion of a critic
Declaim:	to recite poetry loudly and with feeling

Poetic Licence

Objectives

This unit will help you to:

✓ understand what is meant by 'poetic licence'
✓ appreciate how particular letter combinations can be used in poetry to create certain sounds
✓ avoid confusing some words which have related meanings
✓ see how a poet can use punctuation
✓ practise spelling some difficult words

Section A Guidance

Poetic licence

Poetic licence means 'a departing from strict rule or fact for sake of effect'. The departures from the rules which are very common in poetry are:

- incomplete sentences; abnormal sentences

- unusual word order

  Novels, short stories, essays, reports and other prose writing are based on sentences. Poetry, however, is not. Poetry may contain normal sentences, but often it does not and it does not have to. The poet is allowed to play with words and phrases to create whatever effect he wants to. Poets concentrate on nouns, verbs, adjectives and adverbs – words which convey ideas and images. Prepositions, conjunctions and grammatical forms are not as important for the poet, because they do not usually add very much to the emotional or visual appeal of the poem and they restrict the poet's freedom. The poetic form allows a whole range of interpretations according to the imagination of both the writer and reader. This creative potential is admired by some whereas others may see it as a lack of precision.

  Read the following poem and answer the questions which follow.

Don't talk to me about bread

she kneads
deep into the night
and the whey-coloured dough

springy and easy and yielding to her will

is revenge. Like a rival,
dough toys with her. Black-brown hands in the belly bringing forth a
  sigh.

117

She slaps it, she slaps it double with fists
with heel of hand applies the punishment
not meant for bread

and the bitch on the table sighs
and exhales a little spray of flour
a satisfied breath of white

on her hand

mocking the colour
robbing hands of their power
as they go through the motions, kneading ...

Hands come to life again: knife
in the hand, the belly ripped open, and she smears
white lard and butter, she sprinkles
a little obeah of flour and curses to stop up the wound.

Then she doubles the bitch
up with cuffs, wrings her like washing
till she's the wrong shape

and the tramp lets out a damp, little sigh
a little hiss of white of white
enjoying it.

E.A. Markham

Questions

1   How do the punctuation and the structure of the lines of this poem differ from normal sentences?

2   What effect is the poet trying to create or what purpose is the poet trying to achieve?

3   In your own words, explain what you think the poem is about.

Punctuation in poetry

Some poems are a series of phrases separated by pauses which may or may not be indicated by punctuation marks. The poet does not have to use punctuation marks like the writer of prose because the end of the line and the rhythm and metre of the verses will create natural pauses. Where punctuation marks occur they have their normal meaning. Read the following poem paying attention as you read to the punctuation and lack of punctuation.

***West Coast sea, Barbados* (for Pablo Armando)**

You do not waste your breath
daily, nightly
With sanded swish
Nor embedded rocky growl
You do not roar like man's jet plane direct from Africa
Nor do you vivify the tired, aching visitors
By whistling past their smarting over salted eyes
By tumbling through their noses' corridors
To blow away the smoke from darkened lungs
Decarbonise their sluggish hearts
And set them zooming along life's unpaved and paved highways

No, you roar
Only when your hungry maw
Craves the delights December offers
Until Easter cries 'Enough!'
You pound on shores, homes, and clubs
You rip the roots of trees

From out your sandy resting place
But after that
You cradle the human body
In a rock-a-bye it scarcely feels
You touch the mind
With bluish, greenish, greyish
Wavelets of delight,
With dancing lights from a sun
Who smiles, and peeps between the leaves of Nature's

You cleanse, massage, relax
The city's tiredness and stress
And flush sweet laughter
From the reconditioned bodies of your guests
And best of all, you beckon visitors and viewers
To watch, and wait, watch
And wait for that so brief, so rare and exquisite flash The
green flash,
The green
Incredible Flash.

Bruce St John

Questions

1   What is the effect of the sparing use of punctuation marks in the poem?

2   Why does the poet actually use some punctuation marks?

3   Write an intelligible poem in eight lines using as little punctuation as possible.

Assignment

Select a piece of poetry which appeals to you. This may be a hymn, a popular song, a dub poem, dialect poetry or any other type.

Prepare a written analysis of your chosen piece of poetry and explain to the class what is appealing in it – its sound, its emotional appeal, its rhythm, its message or any other quality. The teacher and the class will discuss all the presentations and make a collection of these poems and analyses for the class library.

**Section B
Language
work**

Language: Sounds and images

Onomatopoeia

This is the use of a word to imitate some natural sound and also the use of words whose sounds give an impression of the sense. For instance, in the words 'hiss' and 'buzz' the last part of the word imitates what a hiss and a buzz are. 'Tick' and 'tick-tock' imitate the sounds of a clock. The word 'ping-pong' (for table tennis) gives an idea of the sounds and sense of the game.

Onomatopoeia has been used by poets throughout the ages. There are some sounds, which, because of the way they are articulated, do give a fair impression of a certain type of noise especially when they are repeated. For example, if you keep on repeating **s**, **sh** and **z** sounds, as in:

> What relish shall the censers send
> Along the sanctuary side!

it creates an impression of sound even if you do not know what the sound is supposed to represent.

The **s**, **sh**, **z** sounds have been used to represent whispering, wind blowing, rivers flowing and many other things.

The **m** sound, which is reminiscent of snoring or deep regular breathing, can be used to suggest peace and quiet.

Poets have also used the **ee** sound and the **i** sound (as in 'tick', 'little') to represent high pitched sounds and therefore whatever makes high-pitched sounds, like birds and consequently happiness, youth, lightness.

The **o**, **a**, **u** sounds (as in 'tog', 'tag', 'tug' are used to represent lower pitched sounds and consequently things like drums, marching, trains, sadness, old age, death, darkness.

In poetry, even if you cannot identify what the sounds are supposed to represent, the sounds of the poem can be appreciated as part of the 'music' of the poem in the same way as the music of songs. Words, therefore, not only have meanings, but they also can 'sound sweet'.

Sentence composition

Cause and effect

Note the relationship between the following:

A is the reason for B.	B is due to A.
A is responsible for B.	B follows from A.
A leads to B.	B is a consequence of A.
A contributes to B.	B is influenced by A.
A results in B.	B results from A.
A causes B.	B is a result of A.

In the previous sentences whether you put A first or B first depends on which one you are really concentrating on.

Word confusion

The close relationship in meaning between certain pairs of words leads people to confuse them even in formal writing. Take, for example, the following pairs of words:

itch/scratch   lend/borrow

teach/learn   imply/infer

In each case the one meaning suggests, leads to or conjures up the other, so the two words in each case are not clearly separated. The problem is remembering which word has which meaning. In order to help your memory, you have to devise a strategy for remembering.

For *scratch/itch*, remember that 'scratch' is used in many different contexts (fingernails scratch, cats scratch, cars get scratches) so it must be 'itch' which means a sensation on a part of your body.

For *borrow/lend*, remember to associate 'borrow' with 'get' and 'lend' with 'give'. Where you have '... me a pen', for example, 'give'(= lend) fits better than 'get'.

For *teach/learn*, remember that teachers 'teach' and pupils 'learn' and that a teacher can teach someone something, but a teacher cannot learn someone something.

For *imply/infer*, remember always to substitute 'deduce' for 'infer'.

Further confusion is created by the English language itself, in which some words can mean both the action and the result of action. E.g.

break

He broke the window. (deliberate action)

The window broke. (result of action)

burn

We are burning the leaves. (deliberate action)

The leaves are burning. (result of action)

Exercise

Choose the correct word to fill each gap.

1 The thorns .... me as I went through the garden. The spots ....
    badly.
        scratch/itch

2 I .... her so much money, that I had to .... some from my mother.
        lend/borrow

3   Having .... all there was to know about engines, I was able to ....
my younger brother how to repair his car.

teach/learn

4   Without being rude, I .... that I thought she was lazy.
Unfortunately she .... my meaning only too easily.

imply/infer

Punctuation

What is the poet's intention when he uses:

- the dashes and

- the dots

in the following poem ?

Parting

We touch – you say goodbye
Then you are gone – vanished.
Like the setting sun – a moment here
Then dusk – twilight – hello night.
But your memory – the afterglow
Lingers on – holds me fixed – thoughtful
And the things said and those unsaid
Chase each other gaily – sadly – raindrops
Flitting down the umbrella of my mind.
Hurry then tomorrow – hurry
That we may meet again ...

Paul Keens Douglas

Spelling

Exercise

Each of the following four-word groups contains one or more words
that are spelled correctly. Choose the correctly spelled word(s).

1   authority   similiar   business   spuntaneous

2   suficient   wheather   intrest   minimum

3   libary   syllabus   embodyeing   pertanent

4   simplified   comunity   facinate   harass

5   appropiate   expedient   benificial   throughly

6   unconsiously   pyschological   asess   adjacent

 7   mortgages   infalible   eradecated   fleuncy

 8   predescessor   obsolete   unimpared   sporadicaly

 9   indespensable   incumbrance   intolerible   intension

10   exibit   critisism   recieved   conspicuous

11   subordonate   transaction   refering   preferebly

12   condemnation   occured   ordinerily   capasity

13   dilligent   statistics   occassion   disguissed

14   unnecessary   whent   suprintendent   curency

15   comtroller   foriegn   resolusion   promotion

16   progressive   reciepts   dependent   seperate

17   apetite   preliminary   concilatory   crucial

18   refrence   pretious   uncertainty   maritial

19   illigetimate   peciular   addressee   rythm

20   enviorment   inditment   seized   scissers

21   araignment   emolument   achievement   dimention

Writing Personal Letters

Objectives

This unit will help you to:

✓ improve the way you write personal letters
✓ use auxiliary verbs correctly in Standard English
✓ expand your vocabulary: the language of politics

Section A Guidance

The letter is one of the oldest forms of written communication. Today the letter is still one of the most important forms of communication in business and between individuals. You will certainly find yourself having to write letters at some time in your life. You should therefore understand how to write letters and how to interpret information in the ones you receive. This is especially so in the case of letters of application and job offers.

Remember too that older relatives and people who cannot read depend on others to read and write letters for them. In such cases, the person puts a lot of trust in you which you should be able to live up to.

Personal letters

When friends and relatives write to each other they do not need to be very formal in the way they set out the letter. Personal letters nowadays are not as popular as they used to be because many people find it easier to use the telephone, which is a more direct means of communication. People also send greetings on special occasions by radio and even television.

Parts of a personal letter

The heading (letter head):	the address of the sender and the date
The salutation:	e.g. Dear Madam, Dear Joyce, etc.
The body:	the message or information
The complimentary closing:	e.g. Yours truly, Yours sincerely
The signature:	the writer's name

Marriage proposals

Up until about the 1950s and even into the 1960s in some parts of the West Indies a young man had to write a letter to the father of a young lady asking his permission to court her. The letter had a fairly set form and in cases where the young lady's parents agreed, they wrote an equally formal reply. The following are examples.

Paria Main Road
Toco

[1939]

Dear Mr and Mrs James

It is with the greatest respect I take upon myself to adress you this letter on behalf of your loving daughter Jane; I hope you will not be offended by my doing so. It is clearly known that a time will come that you have to receive such notice; and now is the time ... It is fully twelve months now since I was watching your daughter; and she was also watching my movements; now the time has come for both of us to reveale our secret ... Mr and Mrs James we are deeply in love with each other; and by her request I write this letter, trusting it will not be in vain. I cannot say much more at present when I shall have learn your intention I will have a plenty to say. I am awaiting your reply at an early date.

Yours Obbdt;

J.H.William

The reply to the proposal:

Toco Proper   [1939]

Dear Mr William

We have received you letter quite safe; I was much surprised when I opened it to see your title ... I had no thought of you whatsoever but I must say that we all is quite glad to know that Jane has made a good choice ... I was always looking at you as a gentleman; as far as I can see; I trust this letter you have written that I might live to see the good result of it; Madam and the sisters also the brothers is quite proud to know that their sister has made a good choice. I hereby give you full permission to visit my place; and when we shall have seen each other we will have some face to face chat; I close with love and respect to you my son ...

Your loving Father and Mother

J.T.James

This exchange of letters was treated as a very serious matter, as you can see from the following comment:

'Each of these letters had affixed to it a two-penny revenue and postage stamp, to indicate its contractual nature, for after an interchange of this kind, failure to carry through the obligation that has been assumed can be taken to the courts by either party, and damages collected. An alteration of the agreement by the young woman or her family will be followed by a demand for the return of any gifts the young man may have made, the value of which is recoverable in law; while the young woman can sue in an action comparable to a breach of promise suit.'

Exercises

1 Imagine you were a well educated person in Toco whom many people admired and trusted, and that Mr William came to you with his letter asking you to improve it (without changing the basic meaning) so that it would give the most favourable impression to the young lady's parents. How would you modify it?

2 Do the same for the parents' reply.

3 Write a reply to Mr William's letter politely refusing his request, giving reasons for your refusal.

4 Imagine you are Jane (the young lady). Write a letter to your parents outlining your position and your wishes.

Love letters

Love letters, on the other hand, have always been written by people, young and old, and are still common up to today. In the West Indies in the nineteenth century letter writing was fairly normal among the ruling class, but because of lack of education among the majority of the population not many people could write. However, Charles Rampini, in his book *Letters from Jamaica* (written in 1873) has preserved for us a 'Batch of Negro letters' and the following letter is one of these.

To Ann Williams   January 25, 1865

My dear Love,

I have taken the pleasure of writing you in time, hopen when it reaches
your hand it may find you at a perfect state of health, as it leaves me at
the present time. I have seeing in your letter, my dear, that you wisch to
know from me if it is true Love from my heart. Dearest love, if it is not
true Love from the deepest part of my heart, whold* [would] I set down
to write you a letter, my Dear? When hear I see they lovely face, my heart
within will burnt; when here I absent from thy face, I long for thy return.
But one thing I did like to tell you again. Do not make it known to the
public before we began. The reason why I say that. I heard a certain boy
was telling me all about it, and that only done by you tellin you feamale
friends, whom cannot help; these one secret must be yours, for this thing
is not known to a soul but I and you and your brother-in-law. Therefor the
fault must be yours. Do not let me hear such thing again from anybody.
My dear love, I will be truly wish that I could be married to you know*
[now], but if my life is spared we shall tark* [talk] further about that. My
dear, pray for me that the Lord will speared my life to become a man, for
I truly wich *[wish] that I and you should be one fleach and one blood. Will
you not like it, my dear love? If you don t wich that, let me know by your
letter. My dear girl, you don t know my love wich I have for you. May the
Lord touch your heart to know these thing wich I now put before you in
this letter. But I must say that I am doing you arm [harm] for taken
such liberty to write you such a letter as this. If it is a liberty please to
let me know by your next letter. Do not send me a note again for a letter.
I can not satisfy when I see a letter wich I can not take me some time to
reed. If you had not paper let me know about in your next letter, and I will
send you some paper. My dear love, at preasant my love for you is so
strong, that I cannot express. So I even write that you may see it. It is
every man deauty* [duty] to write a formil* [formal] letter. My pen is bad
and my ink is pale, but my love will never fail. King Solomon say that Love
is strong as death, and Jealousy is cruel than the grave. Love me little,
bear me longer. Hasty love is not love at all. This is the first time I sat
down to write you about it. I love my Dove. Your love is black and ruby —
the chefer of ten thousand. You head is much fine gold. You lock are
bushy and black as a raven. Your eyes was the eyes in a river, by the
rivers of warter. Your cheeks as a bead* [bed] of spices as sweet flowers.
Your lips is like lilies. Your hand as gold wring. Your legs as a pillar of
marble set upon sockets of fine gold. Your countenance as a Lebenon.
Your mouth look to be more sweet. Your sweet altogether. I have no more
time to write as I am tiard and full time to go to bead. I will now close my
letter with love.

I remain yours truly,

Assignments   **A**   Rewrite the previous letter in modern Standard English, with correct spelling, sentence structure and punctuation. Divide the body of the letter into paragraphs and where verse occurs, set it out in lines as you would a poem.
DO NOT ALTER THE BASIC MEANING OF THE ORIGINAL.

B 1   Write a letter to your teacher seeking permission for and assistance with a Christmas party for the class.

2   Write a letter of invitation to the Headteacher, your class teacher and any other teachers to the party. Ask them to reply.

3   Write a letter to parents asking for contributions to the party and write a thank-you note to those who actually do make contributions.

Section B Language work

Sentence composition

Auxiliary verbs

'would', 'did', 'have', 'had', 'must' are all auxiliary verbs. They have various meanings in Standard English.

would

This has three basic meanings but it is used in several different ways in sentences. The three meanings are:

1   be willing to

2   used to – referring to what has already happened

3   I wish – note though that the use of 'would' with this meaning was more frequent in older English.

Examples – 'used to':

During his playing days he would run five miles every morning.

He would go there every day, even though he did not have to.

Years after my husband died I would still hear his footsteps throughout the house.

The memory was so strong that I would take all sorts of pills to try to forget it.

Examples – 'I wish':

Would that I were lucky.
Would that I had the wings of a dove.

The most common meaning of 'would' is the first – 'be willing to'. However, the problem is not the meaning, but knowing when to use 'would' and when to use 'will'.

- In Standard English 'will' changes to 'would' in reported speech. E.g.

  'I will go' becomes 'I said that I would go'.

- For the sake of politeness 'will' changes to 'would'. E.g.

  Would you please give a donation to a worthy cause?

  Would you close the door, please?

- Because 'would' tends to create ambiguity in reported speech, you may be tempted to use 'will', but you should not. In the statement 'He said that he would come', the past tense form of 'would' suggests that 'that was so then but I don't know if it is still so now'. In spoken English, you might say ' He said that he will come' but it would be incorrect to write this.

do, does

The sentences

  He does come.

  He did come.

  He must be there.

all look like perfectly good English and they are, depending on how you pronounce them or what you mean. In these sentences in English the stress is put on the auxiliary:

  He *does* come.

  He *did* come.

  He *must* be there.

In English 'do/does' and 'did' in sentences like these (which are not negative or questions) are used for emphasis, i.e. to contradict what someone else is saying or suggesting, so

  'He must be here. ' means 'He has to be here.'

In the West Indies in casual speech the sentences are pronounced

  'He does *come.*' meaning 'He comes.'
  [This is not normal in Jamaica]

  'He did *come.*' meaning 'He came.'

  'He must be *here.*' meaning 'He is probably here.'

had

In Standard English 'had' is used when the action in one verb takes place before the action in another. E.g.

I had not seen him before I *saw* him yesterday.

Do not use 'had' simply to mean past tense. E.g.

I had eaten yesterday.

Vocabulary

Expanding your vocabulary

These words will be useful to you whenever you are discussing politics. Study the meanings carefully.

Constitution:	the form of government in a country.
Parliament:	a legislative assembly
Cabinet:	a committee of the ministers of government headed by the prime minister or president
Adjournment:	suspension of a meeting from one day to another
Prorogation:	suspension of parliament from one session to another
Dissolution:	the breaking up of a parliament
Sovereign:	a supreme ruler
Dynasty:	successive sovereigns of the same family
Autocrat:	an absolute sovereign
Ministry:	a department of government
Franchise:	the right to vote
Poll:	a register of voters; an election; voting
Constituency:	the body of voters in one district
Monarchy:	government by a single ruler, usually hereditary
Oligarchy:	government by a few
Republic:	government by the people through representatives usually headed by a president
Anarchy:	absence of government

Writing Letters of Application or Business Letters

Objectives

This unit will help you to:

✓ appreciate the way a business letter is laid out
✓ understand the various parts of a business letter
✓ learn how to write a letter of application
✓ spot mistakes in sentences
✓ choose the most appropriate word for a variety of sentences

Section A
Guidance

Business letters

It is important to be able to understand all the information in a business letter: to know when it was written, who precisely wrote it, whether it is addressed to you alone, whether you are expected to reply, whom you are supposed to reply to, whether something is missing from the envelope, and whether the letter is really for you. An understanding of the parts of a letter and the information in each will help you answer these questions.

Terms and abbreviations in business letters

At the bottom left hand corner of business letters you may see some initials e.g. CH:at. This is the *reference line*. 'CH' are the initials of the person who has signed the letter; 'at' are the initials of the person who typed the letter. This reference line allows the business place to have a record of who typed the letter.

The abbreviation 'Encl' means that there is a paper or document (e.g. a copy of another letter) attached to the letter. This enclosure would have been referred to in the letter.

The letters 'cc' mean that a copy of the letter is being sent at the same time to the persons listed. Here are a few other words which often occur in business letters:

re: a much used short word meaning 'with regard to'.

instant: this word is used in business letters to mean 'the current/ present month'.

RSVP: from the French 'Répondez, s'il vous plaît'. This means that the sender of the invitation is awaiting a reply from you.

Regrets only: this means that the sender of an invitation is expecting a reply from you only if you do not intend to accept the invitation.

Parts of a business letter

Look carefully at the diagram below to see the correct layout of a business letter.

The heading (letter head):	the address of the sender and the date
The inside address:	the name and address of the recipient
The salutation:	e.g. Dear Madam,
The body:	the message or information
The complimentary close:	e.g. Yours truly, Yours sincerely
The signature:	the writer's name handwritten by the writer and the typed name
The reference line:	the initials of both the writer and the typist of the letter

Heading

> New Street,
> Basseterre,
> St Kitts
>
> 21 October, 1990

Inside address

Mrs B. Newcastle
PO Box 4060
Charlestown
Nevis

Salutation

Dear Mrs Newcastle,

Body

I read your advertisement for a holiday special in a tourist magazine. I would like to come and enjoy the water sports and swim in the bay's crystal clear waters. I am also looking forward to seeing the spectacular views of St Kitts across the narrows. I do not own a yacht, so I will not be using the marina. I plan to bring my surf board instead. I also intend to drink a lot of your tropical specials and to order lunch from the open grill.

Complimentary close

Cordially yours,

Signature

Josiah P. Walwyn

Reference line
JW=Josiah Walwyn
ao=Annie Ottley

JW:ao

Letters of application

A letter of application really contains two sets of information – firstly, what is called a cover letter and secondly, what is called a CV. (CV is an abbreviation for the two Latin words 'curriculum vitae'. In the USA a CV is called a 'résumé'. A CV is a summary of a person's education and work experience.)

You may write the cover letter on one sheet of paper and the CV on another one, or you may combine them into one. When the CV occurs separately, it is set out in a specific manner. However, when the applicant's education and work experience are included in a single letter, this information is not necessarily set out in the same way.

The separation of the application into two parts is preferable when the applicant has a substantial education and work experience record, but it is certainly not practical if the applicant does not, or if the record itself may actually prejudice chances of success. Some employers are more afraid of 'over' qualified applicants than under qualified ones and are therefore suspicious of persons with unusual CVs.

Parts of a letter of application

- Start by saying what job it is you are applying for and where you saw it advertised.

- Include information about your education and work experience next, if you are not enclosing a separate CV.

- Now explain how your qualifications, experience, background and intentions which fit you for the job.

- End by requesting a reply and an interview from the prospective employer, if this is appropriate.

The letter should be set out clearly so that it can be easily read and understood. Most school-leavers applying for jobs have no work experience and certificates alone do not convince prospective employers, so your letter of application can be crucial.

Sample letter of application

The following is an application for a job divided into two parts – the cover letter and the CV.

78 Old Street
Pottersville
St Luke

December 13, 1988

Mr O. Turtle
Epson Studios
31 River Road
Newtown
Charlotteville

Dear Mr Turtle,

I am writing to apply for the post of Trainee Artist advertised in last Friday's Herald Newspaper. I plan a career as a graphic artist and I would welcome the chance to work at your Company, particularly as you mentioned the possibility of further training. As the attached résumé shows, I am interested in both Art and English. I think that I have a natural aptitude for art and creative design. One of my hobbies is reading magazines and books to get ideas about designs, colour schemes and fashions. I am prepared to work hard and honestly and to learn whatever the job requires.

May I come for an interview at your convenience? I can be contacted at telephone number 83669.

Yours very truly,

Dwayne Registe

```
CURRICULUM VITAE

Personal Data
Name:  Dwayne Registe
Address:  78 Old Street, Pottersville, St Luke
Telephone no:  83669
Date of birth:  18 September, 1970

Education
Schools
Primary:  St Mary's Prep-School
Secondary:  St Mary's Academy (1981-1988)

CXC General English A   2
CXC General English B   3
CXC General Art         1
CXC General History     3
CXC General Spanish     2

GCE A-Level Art (painting, printing and design)   B

Extracurricular activities
1988: President of debating society
Hobbies:  Reading and music

Work experience
Office Assistant - Fashion Designers Ltd (summer 1987)

References
Mrs G. Blackheart
Manager
Fashions Designers Ltd
5 River Road
Roseau

Sister Elizabeth Antoinette
St Mary's Academy
7 Fields Lane
Roseau
```

Assignment   Using the information in the following letter, write a letter of application in two parts (i.e. covering letter and curriculum vitae). Pay careful attention to punctuation, sentence structure and paragraph structure.

January 11, 1992

Mr Johnny Cake
Frugal Customs Services
Spring Garden Highway
St Michael
BRIDGETOWN

Dear Sir,

My name is Audley Adelphus Moore and I am offering
my services for the position of Customs Clerk you
advertised in Friday newspaper. I just left the
community college and I am looking for a job. I
went to school at Grotto Primary, then St Paul's
Secondary. I got back 2 GCE certificates in English
Literature and Spanish, also Woodwork and History
at CXC. My grades were Literature C, Spanish C,
Woodwork III, History III. I also played football
and joined the debating club and at the Community
College I was also in acting. I got a D in A-Level
Spanish and a C in History. Besides debating and
acting I played cricket and table tennis.

I realise that you want somebody who is ambitious
and that is why I am applying for the job. I do not
have any working experience but I learn very fast.
I really hope you consider me favourably and find
me suitable because I really need a job and I
really am a hard worker. If you want me for an
interview, my address is Retirement Rd., Bay
Pasture, that is right next to the gas station. Two
respectable people who know me are Mrs Cordelia
Brown who was my teacher at St Paul's Secondary and
my Reverend, Fr Johnson at St Paul's Church.

Yours sincerely,

Audley Adelphus Moore

Section B Language work

Sentence composition

Exercise

Correct these sentences if necessary.

1   There are many activist who try to promote dialect.

2   Stress is laid, too heavily on Standard English as used by persons with professions – lawyers, doctors, priest.

3   A job requiring a foreign languages past was required.

4   This teaching method did not fear any better than its predecessors.

5   'Thursday night at the fight' is the name of the programme.

6   Bulletin for all motorist! B.B. has the best auto parts!

7   The children are also thought sentence and verb agreement.

8   You should never entertain that kind of bias argument.

9   Americans refer to them as terrorist simply because they do not like them.

10   'Prosecutor recommends aquittals.'

11   Sociologist and other social scientist have given several explanations for its' presence.

12   Terrorist prefer to kidnapp important dignataries such as journalist, ambassadors and other government ministers.

13   Consider medcine, which has appeared to ease the suffuring of millions.

14   This money could be used for the many poor disadvantage people of the world who are starving and need medical care.

15   Few people, however, have really ever taught of the harm it has brought us.

16   Misfits turn to drugs or alcoholism to relieve the tension they have within them.

17   The government is still fiddling over what to do, but luckily concern groups have taken up the cause.

18   This woman could of had the potential to be of great significance in a household or family.

19   That a feotus is a human being is fully recognisable by scientist.

20   The increase specialisation of labour in the industrialise countries influence young married couples to leave their family and kingsfolk.

21   With reduce spending on these nuclear systems, countries maybe able to persue steady economic and social growth.

22   This war was preceeded by a huge outlay of money by the Axis powers.

23   The United States have remove some of its weapons from European soil and reduce the number of weapons at home.

24   From he was young he had been a member of the First Baptist Church. He helped organised the Men's Bible Class and served as one of the first president.

Vocabulary

Exercise   Choose the most appropriate word to fill in the gaps in these sentences.

1   The apartment will be ready for ... in about a month.
occupation/occupancy/occupance

2   An adopted child needs time for ... to his new parents.
adjust/adjustment/adjustation

3   The Press Association should censure any reporter for the ... of a misleading report.
fabrication/publication/publicity

4   Our attorney will advise you of the amount of ... due to you.
recompense/compensation/expense

5   The manager was widely respected and the players sought his ... whenever they had a problem.
consul/council/counsel

6   A ... for the fire station should be chosen to allow for a quick response to all fires.
site/citation/sight

7   After the ... of her second child the gynaecologist suggested a tubal ligation.
bearing/berth/birth

8   The .... in the world price of oil will bring about an increase in price in everything we use.
rise/raise/raising

9   The ship had lain at ... for two whole days.
anchorage/anchoring/anchor

10   Rumours quickly spread about the ... of his money.
resource/source/resources

Presenting an argument

Objectives

This unit will help you to:

✓ understand what is involved in presenting an argument
✓ use words and sentence structures to make your argument more effective
✓ change the word order in sentences
✓ appreciate how punctuation can be used to strengthen a written or spoken argument

Section A Guidance

What is an argument?

In a conversation or in an essay a person may produce a series of statements, all about the same topic, all intended to convince the listener or reader that the position or opinion being put forward is right, reasonable or true. This is what is called an argument. This use of the term argument must not be confused with its more usual meaning of a dispute or quarrel.

Arguments are a normal part of communication in all areas of life – in religion, politics, morals, law, medicine, physics, biology, chemistry, sociology, economics. Such arguments vary from being very emotional and biased on the one hand to being objective and neutral on the other.

Read the arguments below and answer the questions after each one.

Examinations should be abolished

Examinations only show a child's capability on one specific day. I have seen what exams have done to some children. From the time children do not measure up to their peers academically, they begin to feel inferior. They think it is useless to try in exams as it is their expectation to fail. There must be another alternative to this method of testing which causes so much pain and suffering to those who fail their exams. These children who are looked upon as stupid and dumb are placed under extreme pressures after failing their exams for the first time.

I believe that exams cause children to be nervous, depressed and neurotic. These emotions prevent children from concentrating totally and therefore they prevent the child from attaining the marks he or she is capable of. This fact is exhibited every year in the Common Entrance Examination. Primary school children become so flustered that many of them faint, vomit or even experience black-outs or mental blocks before they sit the examination. As in society, emphasis is placed on the results gained from examinations and not from a pupil's capability as shown by results throughout his school years.

Another problem is that marking is subjective in examinations. This seems to be the feeling of people in reference to the marking of essay questions, where a child has to express himself to a greater extent than in a one-sentence answer. For example, when a pupil writes an essay, that essay may be interpreted in different ways by different examiners. Therefore the result that a pupil receives is based sometimes on luck or on what one specific teacher that marks the paper is looking for.

The most obvious reason why examinations should be abolished is the fact that exams only test how well a child can remember what he has read. This aspect of exams, in my opinion, is rather silly. I cannot see the point in a child memorising work for one specific time and then two hours after the exam is completed the child cannot remember anything. This method of testing is ridiculous. There is no good reason for testing how good a memory a child has. The object of going to school is developing knowledge and understanding, it is not a process whereby children memorise and forget what they are taught.

Exams encourage competition and unhealthy rivalry among children. There is nothing wrong with a little competition, but when this competition turns to rivalry and causes children to turn against each other, it is not at all right. Most children have ambition, but there are others who have a distinct attitude about always being best. This attitude causes very bad characteristics in a child, for if that child does not attain the marks he or she desires, then this causes suicide and drug abuse.

In conclusion, it is my opinion that this unfair system has to be abolished as soon as possible. It is necessary that our children be given a fair chance to prove their capability. As I have witnessed the results of these exams, I feel obligated to do everything in my power to rid our educational system of this injustice.

Questions	1 List the points put forward in favour of abolishing examinations.
	2 Comment on each point and judge whether it is a good point or a bad one.
	3 To what extent is the writer relying on emotion?
Assignment	Write an essay presenting the opposite argument, i.e. 'Examinations should not be abolished'.

The advertising of alcohol should be banned from television

I am convinced that the advertising of alcohol should be banned from television. The impact of advertising is staggering because the combined skill, experience and training of workers in various advertising departments is very persuasive. The true picture concerning the effects of alcohol consumption is not portrayed.

Techniques are devised to jerk viewers into awareness. There is something intrinsically restful and attractive in these idyllic pictures. Yet in reality, the atmosphere has not been quite as calm and peaceful. Have you ever seen an alcoholic beverage being advertised with an undertaker or a street bum, or showing the real danger and potential devastation of alcohol use? Must we continue to be bombarded by false images and misinformation? Television bombards us with the idea that drinking is fun – the men are macho and the women are appealing. We are brainwashed into believing that beautiful people drink and that drinking promotes beauty. The people in advertisements are dressed in expensive fashionable clothes and the background is a romantic setting. They look happy and in perfect control of the situation. This kind of advertising encourages people to drink especially those who are vulnerable. To expose vulnerable and impressionable people – young people and those who are down on their luck – to the advertising of alcohol is nothing short of cruelty.

Television is a very powerful medium. In spite of the high cost of television advertising, alcohol distributors find the opportunities of reaching large audiences in the congenial surroundings of their homes too good to miss. The temptation to exaggerate the qualities of the product is a real one and it is not difficult to see why some advertisements appear to be vulgar or, at least, in poor taste. People may say that we should advertise alcohol because people see alcohol being used anyhow. This is a lame excuse. Although other harmful drugs are being used in our society, their use is not promoted on television.

Now that I have explicitly set out the devastating consequences which alcohol consumption has wreaked on our society, I am sure that you will agree that the advertising of alcohol should be banned from television.

Questions

1   What points does the author give to support his argument that the advertising of alcohol on television should be banned? State each point in a one-line sentence.

2   Identify any words, phrases or sentences in the essay which you think are exaggerating the situation or are emotional. Replace them with more neutral ones.

Assignments   **A**   Imagine that you are the public relations officer for a rum-producing company. What arguments would you put forward in support of advertising alcohol?

B   You are a candidate in an election. Write a speech showing the voters why you are the best person for the office.

C   Look again at the two arguments in this unit. To whom do you think each is presented? Give reasons for your answer.

Class assignment   The class should choose one of the following topics for debate:

- Capital punishment should be abolished.

- Abortion should be legalised.

- All schools should be single-sex schools.

- The use of steroids by athletes should be legalised.

The class should be divided into two groups – one for and the other against the topic. Each group should do the necessary research, prepare supporting arguments and select four speakers to represent it. The debate should take place before the year group and should be judged by a special panel of judges.

Section B Language work

Language: The language of argument

In an argument the arguer has to state his case, he has to strengthen it, he has to try to prove his opponent wrong, he has to concede certain things, he has to compare and contrast, he has to reason, he has to point out causes and results of things. All of these require specific words and types of sentences. For example:

- When you concede a point, you may say 'and still', or words like 'although', 'though'.

- When you point out causes and results, you have to use words/phrases like 'because', 'due to', 'as a result', 'consequently'.

- Words of reasoning are 'therefore', 'hence'.

- Words used to strengthen are 'in addition','besides', 'moreover', 'furthermore', 'too', 'likewise'.

The writer must also be able to use different types of sentences. If you are restricted to a few words and the same types of simple sentences joined by 'and' and 'but', your argument will be dull and unconvincing or make you look very simple-minded. It is equally important for you not to 'decorate'   your sentences with the words mentioned above, because you think they make what you are saying sound impressive.

Sentence composition

Exercise

For each of the phrases below:

i   convert the first word to a noun

ii   change the word(s) following to an adjective and put it in front of the noun

iii use the adjective and noun as the subject of a proper sentence

Example
> 'beat savagely' becomes 'savage beating'

> Sentence: 'The savage beating scarred the boy for life.'

1   accelerate quickly

2   suppose without a point

3   maintain properly

4   appear for the first time

5   speak slowly

6   evade with regularity

7   waste without thinking

8   inform quickly

9   develop from start to finish

10   confuse without hope

11   conclude in a few words

12   contain in all

13   write without paying attention

14   collect with discretion

15   attract specifically

16   revise every night

17   transmit in one direction

18   recognise at once

19   examine without care

20   demolish everything

Punctuation

Pauses in speech and writing

Pauses are used in speaking to allow the hearer to understand which parts of the utterance go together and which are separated, to make the meaning clear, to highlight words or phrases and to impress the hearer.

Note the importance of pauses in the following sentence:

> Fred, where Philip had had 'had had', had had 'had'; 'had had' had had the teacher's approval.

Re-read the sentence until it makes sense to you.

Some pauses are made at points which in writing would be marked by punctuation. Other pauses are made at points which are not marked in writing and which it would be incorrect to mark in writing.

Pauses in speech are made at the discretion of the speaker and are not dictated by rules. The use of punctuation to indicate pauses in writing is dictated by the rules of Standard English.

A pause is usually made after the subject of the sentence when the subject is made up of a number of words. E.g.

> St Elizabeth, St Catherine, St Ann and St James are parishes in Jamaica.

It would *not* be correct in writing to put a comma after 'St James'.

A pause is made after an emphatic adjective or adverb at the beginning of the sentence. E.g.

> Here he stands before you, this brilliant man. Great is his contribution to this country.

It would *not* be correct in writing to put a comma after 'Here' or 'Great'.

A pause may occur at a point where a word is not repeated. E.g.

> Hagler was the harder puncher; Sugar Ray the better boxer.

> To err is human; to forgive divine.

It would *not* be correct in writing to put a comma after 'Ray' or 'forgive'.

A pause may occur after 'or' and 'and'. E.g.

> He may go up there or he may come down here.

> He came for my birthday and I know what he brought.

It would *not* be correct in writing to put a comma after 'or' or 'and'.

Extract from an address to the World Council of Churches by Michael Manley

every man who has ever spent a lifetime at work and never once been asked to help plan next year's production is a victim every woman who has been denied work because of her sex or received unequal pay for her work is a victim every person who has been denied equality who has been treated with less than full regard who has been maimed or killed because of race or religion is a victim every human being who has been imprisoned without genuinely fair trial or denied access to justice in our courts of law because of poverty or ignorance is a victim every nation that is condemned to comparative poverty while a transnational corporation accumulates profits out of its natural resources is a victim liberation is about victims and so long as there is one victim upon the face of the earth the process of liberation must continue

Exercises

1   Punctuate the speech according to the rules of Standard English.

2   Read the speech as if you yourself were addressing the World Council of Churches. Indicate, by using slashes in every sentence, where you would make pauses. Use two slashes (//) for a long pause and one slash (/) for a shorter pause.

Advertising

Objectives

This unit will help you to:

✓ reflect on the purpose and techniques of advertising
✓ analyse various advertisements
✓ see how language is used to make advertisements effective
✓ correct spelling mistakes used in some advertisements

Section A
Guidance

The purpose, effects and nature of advertising

The purpose of advertising

Read this essay and then answer the questions:

Advertising has become one of the most powerful influences in the world today. It influences the choices of all people, especially those in the Western world.

An advertisement is a specific kind of argument intending to make you buy a product or service. Although the purpose of advertising in most cases is to sell a product or a service, public service organisations and governments also advertise to promote social good and to prevent people from doing harm to themselves. For instance, a Heart Association may encourage people to eat better and exercise more, and a service club (such as the Lions, Jaycees) may advise people not to drink and drive. Politicians also use advertising to win votes or support for some issue.

Experts do not agree about the effects of advertising on the consumer. Some believe that consumers are persuaded to buy things that they do not need or can't afford; some believe that consumers are merely given information which they use to choose things, which by and large improve their lifestyle. The former think that as a result of the sheer volume, insistence and repetition of advertisements the consumer succumbs. The latter think that the volume and repetition create apathy and that it is only when the consumer needs something and is impressed by an advertisement that advertising is effective.

In general, advertising provides you with information, which in turn gives you choice. It is for you to decide what to do with the information and how to choose. In comparison with your elders of forty years ago, you now are aware of more products, services, job opportunities and possibilities for recreation.

Advertising benefits you indirectly in some ways. For instance, advertising provides the major part of the money needed to keep a newspaper going, which in turn keeps the price of the newspaper fairly low. Advertising also contributes a major part of the budget of television stations.

In general, it contributes to an increase in commerce, a rise in the standard of living, increase in employment and in the case of the West Indies, the importance of advertising to tourism is quite clear.

Advertising in the form of public relations has become an integral part of most big and some small companies and institutions today. The public 'image' of people and organisations is constantly promoted by involvement in social activities, sponsorship of clubs, sports and performances. Most international sports, including the Olympics and the World Cup, depend on advertising for their continued existence.

A modern world without advertising is inconceivable. In addition, advertisements themselves can be quite artistic and pleasing.

Because the world of advertising is highly competitive, unfortunately advertisers feel free to use all techniques to achieve their aim. This means that today, especially in big countries, extensive research is done to see how best to persuade people to buy a product or do what the advertiser wants them to do. Companies, in an attempt to increase their profits, extend their markets into other countries and transfer their advertisements wholesale, which, if done on a wide scale, can change the culture and life-style of countries which are not big enough to produce their own advertisements. It is important therefore for a country to know how to deal with foreign advertisements and for all individuals to be able to handle advertisements intelligently and to choose in their own interest.

The most powerful persuasive factors in advertising are not language, but things which the normal person does not consciously analyse. Advertisers spend a lot of time deciding on colours, lay-out and comforting associations, whereas the normal person is more aware of sex images and grand claims. Even so awareness does not necessarily mean that the person will not buy the product, because all kinds of images and claims are accepted as normal in advertising. In fact, in the case of familiar products where the aim of the advertiser is chiefly to keep the product in the buyer's mind, since failure to advertise will cause the buyer to forget it, the content of the advertisement is not really so important.

Exercises

1   List all the points given in favour of advertising in the essay above.

2   List all the points which describe the ill effects of advertising.

3   Write two paragraphs explaining what you like and dislike about advertisements.

Different types of advertising

Newspaper advertisement: These are of two main types: there is general advertising and also a section called 'Classified advertisements'. Here individuals can advertise using as few words as possible to keep the cost of the advertisement down. Newspaper advertisements are seen by many people, but they are not long-lasting because the newspaper is quickly discarded.

Magazine advertising: These are usually glossy and pretty, but are not seen by as many people as those in newspapers.

Television advertisements: Most are about thirty seconds long and depend on pictures with spoken and written messages.

Radio advertisements: These of course depend on spoken messages. Radio and television advertisements are forceful but the pictures and voices last only a short time.

Telephone directories: Yellow Pages advertisements are long-lasting but condensed, thereby requiring a greater effort to read.

There are also advertisements on outdoor signs, in shop windows, on vehicles and on the products themselves.

Techniques in advertising

When a product is familiar, what the advertiser tries to do is to keep the product in the consumer's mind. This is done by using slogans. E.g.

>   Coke is it

>   You're the reason we fly

>   We do chicken right

>   Let your fingers do the walking

together with positive associations – smiling faces, young people enjoying themselves, young ladies. In these cases, the words, though carefully chosen, are of secondary importance to the pictures and images.

   When a product is not familiar, the first thing the advertisement has to do is to attract attention. Attention-getting devices may be the layout or some appealing part of the language itself.

Assignment   **A**   Look at the seven advertisements shown here. Comment on each one, using these questions to help you.

1   Does the advert depend on a positive image and a slogan?

2   What kind of image does the advert use? What kind of audience do you think it is trying to influence?

3   Where would you expect to see an advert like this?

4   What do you think of the advert's layout? Does it use different print sizes and types? Which words attract your attention first?

5   How successful do you think the advert is?

B   Using the information in the Gleaner advertisement (Ad. 1), write a short essay explaining the advantages of newspaper advertising over other forms of advertising.

The ACK in the knack of advertising

ACK = Attract, Convince, Keep

Attract: The consumer must be made to see or hear the advertisement by making it different from its surroundings.

Convince: The advertisement must convince the consumer, whether by logic, enticement or threat.

Keep: The consumer must be constantly reminded or caused to remember the product or service by repetition or association.

Repetition is the most used technique in advertising.

Exercises

Use the information in the passages above to answer the following questions. You can use the adverts shown here as examples if necessary.

1   How do advertisements appeal to the consumer? (Answer in about 100 words.)

2   What are some common methods used to persuade the consumer to buy a product or service? (Answer in about 150 words.)

3   What techniques are used to get the consumer to remember products, services and companies? (Answer in about 50 words.)

**Section B
Language
work**

Language: The language of advertising

Some advertisements on television and radio contain catchy songs or jingles which are easy to remember. These songs and jingles can be thought of as popular forms of poetry in which rhythm, rhyme and words blend to give a pleasant appeal.

Poetry also occurs in written advertisements – this is usually because there is rhyme or division into lines which causes the consumer/reader to read the advertisement as if it were poetry. Here are a few examples:

So much more than ever before

a perfume for women
a cologne for men

National Bank and You
Together there's nothing we can't do.

Advertisements also use alliteration (see Unit 11). E.g.

> positive, progressive, purposeful

Vocabulary

Favourite words in advertisements

In addition to the very common and safe words which are the favourites of advertisers. E.g.

> new   special   natural   good   great   rich
>
> fresh   bright   free   clean   safe   real

There are a number of compound words which advertisers, because of their desire to keep sentences short, have made into familiar expressions. E.g.

> top-quality   economy-size   fold-away
>
> long-lasting   all-purpose   multi-purpose
>
> high-speed   built-in   twin-pack
>
> letter-quality   duty-free   fresh-tasting
>
> store-wide   do-it-yourself   sale-priced

Compound words which are hyphenated in this way are so familiar because of advertisements that they are now much more frequently used in all types of writing.

Exercise

Make up an advert, using at least two of the compound words listed above.

Spelling

Exercises

On the following page there are four pictures of signs on which there are spelling mistakes. Under each picture there is a phrase which makes an amusing but meaningful comment about the spelling mistake.

1   Correct the spelling mistake(s) in each picture.

2   Explain what you think each of the comments under the picture means.

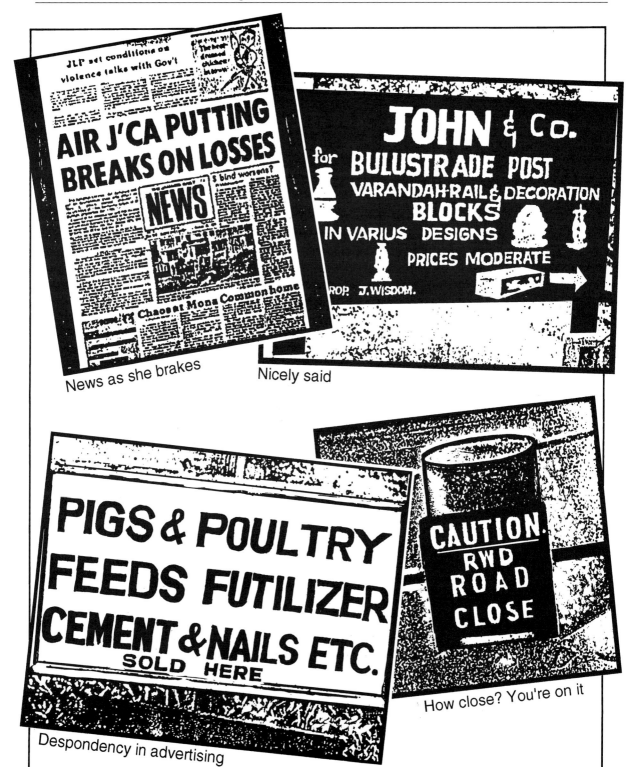

News as she brakes

Nicely said

Despondency in advertising

How close? You're on it

Newspaper Writing

Objectives

This unit will help you to:

- ✓ understand what is meant by 'journalese'
- ✓ analyse the way headlines are made up
- ✓ recognise bias in any piece of writing
- ✓ appreciate the way letters to a newspaper can express people's opinions
- ✓ think about the way the context affects the way we write
- ✓ notice the way some forms of punctuation have become popular

Section A Guidance

'Journalese'

The word 'journalese' is used to describe the style of language found in newspapers. However, it is not easy to say what exactly makes 'journalese'. Here are some possible reasons for the use of the word:

- an impression created by the kind of language used in newspaper headlines

- the tendency towards sensationalism and bias common in many newspapers

- a tendency to make up words and to use punctuation in a creative way

- the belief that since the newspaper has to cater to the average person, the language cannot be too difficult, the sentences cannot be too long, and the content must be made palatable and interesting

- the conclusion that the newspaper account of things is not cold, hard facts but something to be taken with a 'pinch of salt'

Headlines

Newspaper headlines must catch the reader's interest either because they are puzzling, amusing or provocative. There is a difference between the title given to an essay and the headline in a newspaper or magazine. In a normal essay the title gives the topic, but in a newspaper the headline has to attract the reader to read on. Normally headlines have to be short and fit on one line. In order to do this, headlines omit words which the average reader automatically fills in from knowledge of the language and the situation.

The structure of headlines

Headlines are normally of three types:

1 Noun phrases

Language and the press

Race in politics

Record budget

2 A sentence with a present tense verb

A true Christian passes

Policyholders blast Mutual

Transport Board clamps down on reckless drivers

9-year-old tells of assault

3 A clause with a past participle

Magic injured as Lakers lose

Covert action urged in Latin America

3 Arabs shot dead

Over 20 punished for bus accidents

Questions

1   Comment on the headline of the article opposite – would it cause you to read the article? Why/why not? How is it related to the passage?

2   Mr Raspberry uses the words 'new woman' and 'new man'. Why does he use these terms? Why does he use the terms with quotation marks around them?

3   Why does the author start the article talking about himself and his marriage?

4   Pick out the compound (hyphenated) words and say in each case what is the advantage of using a compound word.

5   Give a list of both the virtues and the bad points of the 'old man' and compare them with those of the 'new man'. Why, according to the author, is the new man a flop?

6   Give the meaning of the following words:

fop   modicum   psychically   fishfowl   liability

7   The author likes to use clauses/phrases between commas in sentences (e.g. 'I admit'; 'as you might guess'; 'according to the *Working Woman* article'; 'in short'; 'to be sure'; 'the author complains'). Why does he do this? What effect does it have? Does it make the tone of the passage less formal? Does it make the passage easier/harder to understand?

8   Identify and correct all cases of use of punctuation marks and sentence structure which would be considered incorrect in formal writing.

Where will 'new woman' find a man?

William Raspberry

WASHINGTON - I am ashamed, I admit, of my it-serves-'em-right-attitude. After all, I enjoy a happy marriage, and I'd like to wish the same happiness for others. Still I feel just a little bit like gloating. I've just looked at the May issue of Working Woman magazine, attracted to it by a featured article, 'But Does the New Woman Really Want the New Man?' The answer, as you might guess, is a frustrated - no.

But why does that make me feel, if not good, at least psychically vindicated? I suppose it's because I have long thought that the feminists were playing on dangerous ground. It made sense to me that they wanted to get rid of the gender-specific constraints that had limited women's economic options. It was the next step that made me nervous: that women couldn't be really free unless men also were freed of their gender-specific roles and attitudes. The success of feminism, in short, would require the creation of a 'new man.'

There was, to be sure, plenty wrong with the 'old man.' He was inconsiderate and possessive; he tended to define himself by the kind of work he did, and to think of the woman in his life as 'his.' But just as novice remodellers, in their zest to turn their 'handyperson special' into a dream house, sometimes make the mistake of removing load-bearing walls, the architects of the 'new man' may have eliminated some of his key supporting timbers. The result, according to the Working Woman article, is something nobody wants.

He's no longer possessive, say Margaret Edwards, a University of Vermont associate professor of English, but he is no longer committed. He has given up the notion that the man should make all the decisions, but women find it frustrating that he can't make up his mind what the couple should do or where they should eat, or even whether to ask her for a date. He neither opens doors nor sends flowers. He has, the author complains, been transformed 'from tyrant to fop.' Or flop.

Feminists understood clearly that the traditional feminine attributes (cooperativeness, peace-seeking, self-denial) put them at a career disadvantage vis-à-vis men with the traditional masculine characteristics (aggressiveness, assertiveness, competitiveness). But they also understood that it would solve nothing for women simply to start behaving like men – if only they could play that role as well as men.

So they came up with the notion that men, too, would have to change: to become more like women. The 'new man' thus created turns out to be a fishfowl that nobody wants. As Edwards puts it: "Women don't yet admire in men what have been known as the 'feminine virtues.' It took women so long to get out from under these virtues that one can hardly blame them for still being suspicious of them."

The mistake, which Edwards doesn't acknowledge, was not in recognizing that while 'feminine virtues' can be a handicap in male-dominated careers, they can be an enormous help in forming strong personal relationships, because they encourage men to do what they are best equipped to do: behave like men. The 'new man,' Edwards acknowledges, is a frustration. 'He accepts that women have joined him on the fast track, yet their paths seem to be parallel, not intersecting.'

Her proposed solution is unlikely to please very many men or women.

'The New Woman,' she says, 'will have to look past the classic knight on the white charger to find the next hero. . . She may have to take a chance on living with the type of man who benefits from her energy rather than duplicates it, who admires her clear sense of purpose and doesn't thwart it, who feels inclined not so much to lead her as to enjoy where she leads. 'Right now, her heaviest liability is a likelihood of winding up alone.'

With practice, a little counselling and a modicum of consciousness-raising, I'm sure I could learn to stop murmuring: It serves her right.

William Raspberry is a *Washington Post* columnist

Assignment

You are the editor of a newspaper. Work out a plan for a controversial and provocative lead article.

Understanding bias

It is important that you are able to recognise bias in a newspaper article or any piece of writing. We are all biased.

When something happens to people in a distant community we can sit back and make harsh comments about it, but when it happens to us we see things in a much more sympathetic way. As well as this individual bias, there are attitudes to other cultures, which one can call *cultural bias*. These attitudes are reflected in the words we use. For example, the two words 'religion' and 'superstition' have similar meanings, but their connotations are quite different: the word 'religion' is very often used to refer to the beliefs of powerful and wealthy societies; while 'superstition' is used to refer to the beliefs of poorer societies. For instance you are made to believe that Catholicism is a 'religion' while voodoo in Haiti is a 'superstition'.

Consider the bias and emotion in the words in the following lists:

Negative bias	*Positive bias*
foolhardy	brave
licence	freedom
terrorist	freedom fighter
stubborn	firm
queer	quaint
self-seeking	ambitious
fanatic	pious

Exercise

By looking at copies of various newspapers, find an article which seems to you to be biased. Select the words used in the article which are evidence of this.

Letters to the editor

Writing a letter to a newspaper is a good way of expressing one's opinions. Read this example.

Dear Editor,

I write this letter in response to the recent debate on the banning of dub music on the minibus. My position is that dub music should not be banned.

Dub music is appealing to young people and the majority of passengers on the minibus are young. This is a democratic society and the minority will have to give way to the majority. Dub music is the current form of musical entertainment and people will have to move with the times. Calypsos and rock and roll had their opponents when they were new on the scene. In the same way that they have become accepted, dub will also become accepted with exposure.

In my opinion, the rhythm of the dub music in the morning helps to wake up the passengers on their way to work and school, and in the evening it helps to calm their nerves after a hard day. The advantages of having dub on the minibus far outweigh the disadvantages. I strongly oppose those conservative and insensitive people who want the world to remain as it was when they were young and oppose whatever the young people of today do. Keep dub on the minibuses.

Dubby Dub

Exercise

Write a letter to the editor in answer to Dubby Dub, expressing your opinion that dub music should not be played on minibuses.

Section B Language work

Language: The context of argument

Because behaviour has to be appropriate for the time, place and people involved, context has a strong influence over the kind of language that must be used in a given situation. For example, if a Christian teacher were presenting Christ's resurrection to her Sunday school class, she would not present it in the same way as she would if she were addressing a group made up of scholars from many different cultures and religions. A teacher of the first class in primary school does not use the same types of words and sentences as a teacher of a sixth form.

According to the audience, an argument may be friendly, businesslike, literary, legalistic, technical or learned.

Friendly arguments tend to make use of exaggerations with superlatives (most, best, only, worst).

Legalistic arguments make points but keep on referring to definitions and previous instances which are similar or dissimilar.

Literary arguments make use of metaphors, similes, 'learned' words and idiomatic expressions.

Technical arguments carry the jargon of the subject, which makes them difficult to follow.

Punctuation

The popularity of colons and dashes

Colons and dashes are very popular with writers nowadays, especially in newspapers and advertising.

Colons are popular because lists and direct quotations, both of which colons are used to introduce, are more graphic and striking ways of presenting information.

Dashes are popular because they are so versatile. They attract the attention of the reader by visually separating one word or set of words from another, as well as allowing the reader to separate one idea from another. Dashes are especially common when full sentences are not being used, as in news headlines, notes and advertisements.

The purists say that dashes are imprecise and do not require much thought from the writer. Using too many dashes in your work will give your work an informal look and tone. You should not try to escape from precise punctuation (full stops, commas, colons) and variety in the length of sentences by resorting to dashes.

The colon is used when the words following are a list, a phrase summing up, a quotation, an illustration or an explanation. It usually comes after 'as follows:' and '... the following:'. E.g.

> This involves far more than the correct formation of letter shapes: letter sizes, word spaces, spaces between lines, margins, and other matters of layout also need to be consistent, if a writing style is to be acceptable.

The dash is used to set off qualifying information or explanation in the same way that brackets are used. It is used when the words following sum up the sentence, or with the colon to introduce lists or when the words preceding are only part of the sentence. E.g.

> Many people who are not trained in touch-typing – including children, programmers and journalists – are fast hunt-and-peck typists.

> Children have to learn a range of linguistic skills – reading, writing and spelling.

Exercises

1   Get a copy of a newspaper. Pick out ten examples of colons and ten examples of dashes. Explain in each case what the colon or dash is being used to do.

2   Insert colons, where appropriate, in the following:

  i   All that and I must leave it at that is the background against which I have to operate.

  ii   With intellectual growth the child breaks away from this kind of simple analysis and turns to functional analysis what things can do or what a person can do with things.

  iii   Three components of memory are identified memorising, storage in the memory and reproduction. One can further distinguish between two types of memory arbitrary and non-arbitrary.

  iv   You are invited to attend the 13th dub.

> On stage R-dub, U-dub, B-dub
> Time from sunset you say when
> Dress Rub-a-dub style

Writing Reports or Exam Answers

Objectives

This unit will help you to:

✓ know what is meant by expository writing
✓ make the writing up of scientific experiments clear and comprehensive
✓ see how analogies can be useful
✓ practise writing effective sentences
✓ spot correct spellings

Section A Guidance

Expository writing

Essay questions on an exam paper, reports on research projects, news items and bulletins and the writing up of laboratory experiments, all involve the presentation of information in what is called 'expository writing' or 'exposition'. This kind of writing is normal in school, business, government and the media. In expositions you have to manage

• the subject matter

• the structure

• the language

Organising your writing

You may know a lot about a certain subject but if you do not organise your exam answer or report well, you will not convince your reader that you know what you are talking about. On the other hand, good organisation and clear language may convince the reader that you are intelligent and knowledgeable, even when in fact you do not know very much about the subject.

At the outset, you need to be able to identify the kind of writing which is required of you. Consider the following instructions:

1 Let me have a report on this on my desk by tomorrow.

2 Write short notes on the following ...

3 Discuss the advantages and disadvantages of ...

4 Explain the difference between ...

5 Say in your own words what happened.

Interpreting such instructions may seem obvious, but experience shows that people do what they want to do rather than what they are asked to do. In other words, disregard of instructions is by far the most common fault in answering questions.

Exposition is different from presenting an argument. In an argument the writer is intent on trying to change the reader's attitude. In a piece of expository writing your main aim is to give clear, coherent information about something.

Writing up science experiments

Some science students do not think that English is a part of science, but it should be made quite clear that if you write up your experiments and your teacher cannot understand what you did, you will suffer the consequences. Poor writing in science subjects creates misunderstanding, misinterpretation and possibly costly mistakes.

Headings to indicate the different things which you did or which happened are an integral part of lab reports:

AIM
The purpose/objective should be clear to the writer and reader. In lab reports this must be clearly stated.

APPARATUS
Note all the instruments, materials and objects involved. This is the first step in observation.

METHOD
Note what was done. Sometimes how and when it was done are important. This is the second step in observation.

RESULT
Note the changes that took place. Sometimes what did not take place is important. This is the last step in observation.

CONCLUSION
This requires knowledge of the subject and thought. Giving reasons, causes and effects is not a matter of flashes of brilliance, it is a matter of previous steady work, careful observation and understanding.

It would be good if such headings were required in all subjects, as fundamental training, even if they were dispensed with later in some subjects.

Any report should begin with a *statement* of the task (i.e. what you aim to do). Depending on the length and nature of the report, you may have to state the newness of your method and your limitations. The *body* of the report is made up of an explanation of the apparatus and materials, what you did, the methods you used, the results (i.e. what you observed) and a discussion of the results.

The following is a report on an experiment by a biology student.

Germinating seeds and respiration

AIM
To see whether energy is released by germinating seeds

APPARATUS

2 flasks	seeds
2 thermometers	vaseline
2 rubber bungs with delivery tube	lime water
2 test tubes	
1 beaker	

METHOD
The live seeds had been in the water previously, germinating. The water was poured off them and they were placed in a flask. Some other seeds had been boiled to make sure that they were not living and then they were put into Chlorox bleach, in order to kill off any possible bacteria which would give a false reading.

   The dead seeds were put into another container by themselves. Both flasks were stoppered with rubber bungs connected to delivery tubes and vaseline was put around the stopper to prevent any air from getting inside. Some lime water was placed in two test tubes and the bottom of each delivery tube was put into the lime water.

OBSERVATION

Date & time		Temperature	
		Living seeds	Dead seeds
93-05-13	12 noon	31°C	31°C
	12:45 pm	32°C	31°C
93-05-14		33°C	31°C
93-05-15		33°C	31°C

On the first day the lime water turned milky in the case of the live seeds and there were bubbles present which were coming out at a fast rate.

   The lime water turned milky on the fourth day in the case of the dead seeds and there were some bubbles present which were coming out quite slowly.

CONCLUSION
We can conclude that respiration did take place as shown in the equation below. Energy was given out in the form of heat from the living seeds as signified by a rise in temperature. The lime water also turned cloudy which shows that carbon dioxide was present. The dead seeds were used as a control showing no significant change.

$$C_6H_{12}O_6 + 6O_2 \longrightarrow 6CO_2 + 6H_2O + energy$$

glucose   oxygen   carbon   water
                           dioxide

Assignment   Three science students should be assigned to present three different laboratory reports to the class. As the students present their reports, the other members of the class should judge them using the following guidelines.

1   Are the aims clearly stated?

2   Are the materials and methods listed?

3   Are the observations clearly described?

4   Are the conclusions clearly stated and related to the aims?

5   Are the explanations and discussions plausible?

In order to help the whole class to understand, presenters should give written explanations of scientific jargon.

Section B Language work

Language: Using analogies

In order to explain a concept which is difficult, a writer may use an analogy (i.e. a comparison) with something which is familiar. For instance, in literature a poet has been compared to an albatross (a sea bird). The idea is that when the albatross is soaring high in the sky, it is magnificent and in a class by itself, but when it lands on the shore or on a ship, it looks extremely awkward. In the same way, the poet deals with thoughts, ideas, emotions and language in a lofty and spiritual manner, which, when measured against real and everyday material things, may seem out of place and useless.

Some social science subjects have used concepts from biology. A simple example is the concept of the family 'tree'. Here the structure of a tree with its branches (drawn upside down) is used to show the relationship between father and mother, children, grandchildren, cousins, uncles, aunts, etc.

Sentence composition

Exercises   A   For the following five questions, use the information given in brackets to make one sentence, beginning your answer with 'It is/was'.

1   Who climbed Mount Everest? (Edmund Hillary, some years ago.)

2   Was Columbus the first European to come to the West Indies? (No, Miss Piggy was the first person to sail across.)

3   When and how did man first land on the moon? (In a balloon. It burst and flew away in 1905.)

4   During slavery how did the slaves get money? (The masters for whom they worked allowed them to plant crops and sell them.)

5   What was the most difficult thing to do after Emancipation? (To stand on one's head and drink water from a calabash. No straws were available.)

B   In each of the following convert the two sentences into one. Do not change the order of the sentences. Do not use *and* to join the sentences. Do not change the meaning.

1   You cannot go. You have to face that fact.

2   You did not pass the test. That is the verdict.

3   Where did he go? That is the mystery.

4   Are you really upsct? I wonder.

5   There are only two days left. I am excited.

Spelling

Exercise

Identify the correctly spelled word in each of the following groups.

1   calender   maintainance   analysize   indefinite

2   anonymus   personnel   intension   appropiate

3   labratory   occassional   alledge   privilege

4   acknowlege   beneficial   stastistics   garantee

5   pronounciation   intelligence   unconcious   ridecule

6   incooperate   ocurrence   corporation   pregnansy

Organising Information

Objectives

This unit will help you to:

✓ organise your information when writing exam answers or reports
✓ write clearly and objectively
✓ use the noun style effectively
✓ identify the correct word in a series of sentences
✓ spell local words correctly in factual writing

Section A Guidance

There are at least four patterns which you can use to organise and structure your subject matter/information, when writing exam answers or reports:

• time

• space

• topic

• step-by-step

Time pattern

A time pattern is fairly straightforward and lets the reader follow what you are saying quite easily. The times which you deal with may be minutes/hours/days/years/eras. E.g.

at 7.30 ...   at 8.15 ...   at 9.03 ...   in 1986 ...   in 1987 ...

in 1991 ...   in the early period ...   in the middle period ...

in the late period ...

In the following paragraph note how the writer moves forward from year to year:

The silver men (1)

Competition on the United Kingdom markets forced West Indian sugar producers to look elsewhere. From the 1870s, they found an expanding market in the United States, where, by 1883, 104,642 of a total production of 224,450 tons were sold. The amount increased until 1898, when competition from Cuban and Puerto Rican sugars, following the Spanish American War, caused a sharp decline. For example, the value of sugar exports from Barbados to the United States declined from £354,875 in 1901 to £292,131 in 1902, and then slumped to £51,502 in 1909. To some extent, the contraction of markets in the United Kingdom and the United States for British West Indian sugar was counterbalanced by an increase in sugar exports to Canada. These rose from 1000 tons in 1897 to 133,000 tons in 1909, and were still rising by 1914.

Space pattern

Space can in a strict sense be related to points of the compass (i.e. north, south, east, west). However, in a looser sense it means that the writer is moving systematically from one place to another. A writer can move your vision gradually from left to right or from top to bottom depending on his overall intention.

Note the movement from one set of islands to another in the following paragraphs:

The silver men
(2)

The crises of 1846 and 1847, and the steady decline in sugar prices on the United Kingdom market after 1874, ruined many sugar interests in the West Indies. By 1900, many of the commercial houses financing sugar production in the islands had collapsed.

The results were far-reaching. In Barbados and St Kitts, no estates were abandoned but some amalgamations to form more economically viable units occurred, and a few bankrupt estates were subdivided and sold to eager, land-hungry labourers. In Barbados also, estates were said to be experiencing 'a universal loss' by 1900. In other islands, particularly in Antigua, Jamaica, St Lucia and Trinidad, abandonment, amalgamation, diversion of sugar lands to other crops and to grazing pens, and subdivision for sale or rental, all reduced the number of estates producing sugar. In Antigua, sugar estates were reduced from 107 in 1865 to 53 in 1900; in Jamaica from 513 in 1846 to 140 in 1896; in Trinidad from 110 in 1865 to 56 in 1900. Altogether, sugar estates in the British West Indies decreased from 2,200 at Emancipation to between 750 and 800 in 1900.

In a spatial pattern the writer may move from whole to parts and then go through the details of each part to give a complete detailed description. The following passage is an example of such movement.

The St Paul's
gazebo

This unusual building stands in the grounds of what used to be the rectory of St Paul's, just behind the church itself, and not far from Bay Street. It is an irregular octagon, with the length of each side varying from 6' 8" to 6' 10 ½" on the exterior, and from 5' 1" to 5' 6" on the interior, and all the other measurements seem to vary slightly on the different sides. The height from the ground to the top of the outside wall is approximately 14' and from the ground to the top of the pinnacles about 17' 9". There is a fairly recent wooden ceiling, covered on the outside with galvanise (though the original roofing was presumably of shingles), and the inside height from the floor to where the ceiling slopes up to a point is about 12' 10".

Four of the walls are blank. That on the side nearest the rectory has a doorway (about 8' 8" in height from the floor to the top of the arch, and 3' 11" wide at floor level) which is connected to the ground outside by a single low step. The wall opposite the doorway, and the two at right angles to the line so formed, are pierced by windows whose outside width varies from about 3' 7" to 3' 9" at the bottom, and which are 7' 2 1/2" to 7' 3 1/2" in height from the sill to the point of the arch. The height of the sill above ground varies from 2' 2 1/2" to 2' 10". All the openings are slightly larger on the inside than on the outside. Much of the plaster on the inside has come off, revealing that the arches are constructed of brick, with the intervening walls made of rubble stone. Two of the eight pinnacles have been broken, and the remaining stumps show that they are at least partly brickwork. There are drip-mouldings over the door and windows, and a cornice runs round the top of the building.

The space pattern is only a starting point. The full description of an object involves more than movement from part to part, but it is important that you get accustomed to orderly movement which involves following a plan. Use the following as a plan for describing:

- definition

- location

- shape and size

- colour, weight, texture

- main parts

- function

Remember that not all these will be relevant in all cases.

Topic pattern

Topics are ideas/thoughts organised in a unified way with some common factor running through them. This is the most difficult exposition pattern, because whereas movement across time and across space is generally easy to follow, deciding on the importance of topics and the relationship between topics is more dependent on the writer's preferences and intelligence. However, this does not mean that a topic pattern is unachievable. On the contrary, competence/ability in organising ideas is regarded as one of the most important objectives in education. In other words, to be able to put together your thoughts and to move the reader from topic to topic and to conclude logically is the very essence of what an educated person hopes to achieve, whether one is dealing with simple topics or difficult technical or moral ones.

The following passage is an example of a topic pattern.

Use of sugar-cane as livestock feed

The sugar-cane plant can be used for feeding ruminants in two ways: as sugarfith, the name given to the product after a sugar-cane stalk is passed through a machine that removes the hard outer rind; and chopped cane, in which the whole sugar-cane plant (including the cane tops) is chopped, utilising conventional forage chopping equipment. Existing research has not demonstrated any significant difference between sugarfith and chopped cane in terms of animal performance. This, together with the fact that the derinding technology is still in its developmental stage, suggests that chopping is the process most likely to find commercial application at least in the near term.

The advantage of sugar-cane as an animal feed stems from the plant's very efficient photosynthetic ability, resulting in very high yields of convertible energy per hectare and the fact that such energy is available during the dry season when production of traditional forages tends to be low or non-existent. This means that a livestock enterprise based on sugar-cane could afford much higher stocking densities than that permitted with common pasture grasses – available data suggesting stocking rates of 8–10 animal units per hectare compared to 2–3 on improved pasture. Sugar-cane also ensiles well, indicating that the crop can be harvested during the period of its highest nutritive value and conserved for year-round use. Interestingly too, the acceptability of the sugar-cane ration to ruminants is increased when molasses is added as a supplement. Sugar-cane as a major ingredient of animal ration is thus also significant from the perspective of the linkages it creates within the agricultural sector itself.

The step-by-step pattern

The step-by-step pattern is related to the time pattern in that in the step-by-step pattern one thing happens in sequence after another. The emphasis in the step-by-step pattern, however is not on time but on the steps that must be followed to complete a task. It is a matter of reaching a target by following a procedure or going through a process in which the order in which things happen is important. In other words, you cannot do the last step before you do the first. Laboratory experiments, recipes, directions for assembling toys and other items, all involve the following of a step-by-step pattern.

Exercises

1   Using the step-by-step pattern explain to someone whom you are teaching how to solve the following mathematical problem:

$$2 + 6 - 3 - (10 + 14) \times 4$$

2   You are the secretary to a club (choose the type) which is planning an overseas tour. The club is meeting next Friday, at which time you are expected to set out for club members the itinerary of the tour. Write a plan of what you are going to tell the club members.

3   You are taking a short-cut through a lonely area when you come upon a man who seems either drunk, ill or dead. You continue on home, but you decide that you should tell someone who might be able to help. Describe the place as well as the condition and appearance of the man so that the person will know what best to do.

Assignment

Out of every four students one should use the time pattern, one the space pattern, one the topic pattern and one the step-by-step pattern to write a two-paragraph exposition on one of these subjects.

1   The development in tourism over the last thirty years in a Caribbean territory

2   The gaining of independence by territories in the Caribbean since 1960

3   Caribbean-wide institutions

4   The improvement in the rights and privileges of women in the Caribbean

5   Solving a specific mathematical problem

Each of the four students should then read their presentation to the class.

Section B
Language
work

Language: Writing clearly

In order to express yourself clearly and objectively on any topic, you first have to have

- accurate knowledge of the subject matter

- command of the terms and expressions of the subject

- an ability to use objective language

- experience of writing with precision

The most common way of disguising ignorance of a subject is vagueness. Therefore, in order to be able to write well on a subject, you have to be familiar with the subject matter. In doing this, you will automatically come to know and remember the terminology of the subject, what is called the jargon. If you are writing on English literature, for example, you will come to know and use terms such as theme, plot, style, story-line. If the subject matter is biology, you will come to know and use terms such as vertebrate, monocotyledons, photosynthesis, organism.

Objective language should be unbiased and impersonal. An explanation of the structure of a plant in a biology book will not normally contain words such as 'I', 'you', 'good', 'bad', 'believe', 'think', because such words are personal and suggest that the writer is giving opinions. In English the style favoured in presenting factual information is the 'noun' style, with passive verbs and sentences of varied structure and length. A succession of short, simple sentences gives the impression that you are simple-minded and cannot rise to the level of abstraction which the 'noun' style conveys. Remember that the 'noun' style means that the majority of the sentences, not all, have 'converted' nouns with qualifying words and phrases. E.g.

> Better agricultural methods prevent soil erosion and loss of fertility.

Sentence composition

Verb style and noun style

A writer has to choose his words and decide on the structure of his sentences. In your writing you should work out the best way of saying things by trying different ways. E.g.

> He went down the road quickly.

> Quickly he went down the road.

> Down the road he went quickly.

From these sentences you will see that you can change the order of the words in the sentence to give a slightly different tone to the sentence in each case. Some writers prefer a 'noun' style rather than a 'verb' style because it makes what they are writing sound more learned.

Note the difference between:

- verb style – He wanted me *to decide* before he returned.

- noun style – He wanted my *decision* before his return.

Another difference between a 'noun' style and a 'verb' style is that when you use a 'verb' style you will end up with many short sentences, separate or joined by words like 'and' and 'but', whereas when you use a 'noun' style it may result in longer complex sentences.

Exercise   Identify which of these pairs of sentences is written in verb style and which in noun style.

1   He knew I did not like it but this did not stop him from doing it.
His knowledge of my displeasure did not stop his behaviour.

2   He stayed in the spacecraft for a long time and drank no water.
During his long stay in the spacecraft he drank no water.

3   It is that very time that he died.
That is the exact time of his death.

4   When he died he had a fortune.
At the time of his death he had a fortune.

5   Stop where the two roads meet.
Stop at the road junction.

6   When he grew up he became very pleasant.
In his adult years he became very pleasant.

Vocabulary

Exercise   Choose the correct word to complete the following fourteen sentences:

1   The film *The Karate Kid* was such a great success that they brought out a ... .
(i) sequel   (ii) series   (iii) serial

2   You will have to ... that rats and mongooses cannot get at the chickens.
(i) assure   (ii) ensure   (iii) insure

3   There has been a price ... in gas every month for the last eighteen months.
(i) rise   (ii) raise   (iii) raised

4   I am a thousand times better now. The advice which you gave me turned out to be ... .
(i) valued   (ii) valuable   (iii) invaluable

5   The judge in any dispute is supposed to be an ... person.
(i) interesting   (ii) uninterested (iii) disinterested

6   The recording company set up operations in an old, ... sugar factory.
(i) disused   (ii) misused   (iii) useless

7   His previous record ... against his selection for the post.
(i) militated   (ii) mediated   (iii) mitigated

8   Whenever the two boxers got into a ... the referee parted them.
(i) clinch   (ii)   clench

9   Tyson, the heavyweight champion, ... to the left, then to the right and unleashed a savage right hook.
        (i) fainted   (ii) feinted

10   It was feared that in the union elections all the members from the shop floor would vote as a ... .
        (i) block   (ii) bloc

11   As soon as the Queen enters, give him his ...to begin the procession.
        (i) cue   (ii) queue

12   The work of art was done on cardboard and not on ... .
        (i) canvas   (ii) canvass

13   When he was required to be ... after the confidential meeting he was not.
        (i) discreet   (ii) discrete

14   The ... leg was amputated before the gangrene spread any further.
        (i) deceased   (ii) diseased

Spelling

West Indian words in factual writing

There are many West Indian words for which there is a Standard English equivalent and there are also many West Indian words which, although difficult to replace, are not now acceptable for formal writing (e.g. 'jook', 'stupse/chupse'). However, there are words which refer to specific items in West Indian culture and food, items which West Indians talk about in their everyday lives, but for which there seems to be no agreed spelling. This is unfortunate, for students come to believe that what they are familiar with either is not worth writing about or cannot be written about in formal writing. In the same way that once upon a time English spelling was not fixed but gradually became so, West Indians have to believe that the spelling of West Indian words which may not be fixed now will become fixed in the future. The most important fact to remember is that an agreed spelling is for purposes of writing; an agreed spelling cannot and will not reflect the pronunciation of all speakers.

Here are spellings of West Indian items which you should follow:

jumbee	jouvert	papaw	kumina	cou-cou	cerasee
matty	ackee	corbeau	ginep	obeah	funji
jonkanoo	bammy	conkee	diable	chenette	ligarou
okra	calaloo	Anancy	paymee	guepe	jimbling
dungs	tannia	duckanoo	duppy	diablesse	

Note the following words, which are Caribbean words (from the original native population), and which today occur in the English language with an agreed spelling:

Arawak & Carib:	*Aztec:*	*From Honduras:*
barbecue	cocoa	mahogany
canoe	chocolate	
hurricane	tomato	
maize	avocado (pear)	
potato		
tobacco		
hammock		
iguana		

Note also the following words from Hindi and Chinese, languages of the fore-parents of some West Indians:

Hindi:	*Chinese:*
bungalow	tea
khaki	silk
shampoo	tycoon
dungaree	
jungle	
loot	
pyjamas	

Exercise

Choose ten words from the list of West Indian words given above. Learn the agreed spelling and then include each in a sentence.

Following Directions and Instructions

Objectives

This unit will help you to:

✓ complete forms efficiently
✓ write and follow a series of instructions
✓ interpret information given in statistical tables
✓ obtain information from maps and plans
✓ use descriptive phrases
✓ understand how instructions and explanations use different words and structures

**Section A
Guidance**

In this unit we will be looking at aspects of language which affect everyday life, such as filling in forms, following instructions, giving and understanding directions and interpreting statistical tables/graphs.

Completing forms

There are many occasions when you will need to fill in a form, e.g. for a birth registration and certificate, a passport and identity card, a driver's licence, income tax calculation, an insurance policy, a death certificate. Many people have difficulty with forms and this means that forms are often returned incomplete. This failure to complete forms properly is usually a matter of not understanding the instructions on the forms or not being able to give a precise and correct answer in the space provided. Most of the problems with the completion of forms can be avoided if right from the start the person remains calm, and goes from question to question in a patient, methodical manner until the form is complete.

If you are applying for a visa to go to another country or applying to get into a college, you may be asked to supply details of your personal and private life. You may not get the chance of an interview, so the information you write on the form will determine whether you succeed or fail. It is important therefore that you read each instruction carefully and write in the information required legibly and accurately. When you do not understand what information is required, ask for help.

On some forms you not only have to write in information but also choose from a number of alternatives e.g. Mr/Mrs/Ms. Follow the instructions and cross out the ones which do not apply to you, or tick the one that does. Some forms ask questions which do not apply to you. In such cases it is advisable to write N/A or 'not applicable'.

Some forms have carbon copies. In order to produce legible copies, press hard while you are writing. If you make a mistake remember to correct the carbon copies as well as the top sheet.

INTERNATIONAL E/D CARD

1. Mr.
    Mrs.
    Miss _____
                        Name in full (Please Print)

2. Date of Birth _____
                    (Year)   (Month)   (Day)

3. Country of Birth _____ 4. Nationality _____

5. Occupation _____

6. Home Address _____

7. For all Departing Passengers: Port of Disembarkation _____

8. For all Arriving | (a) Port of Embarkation _____
    Passengers |
                       | (b) Intended Address _____

9. For non-Resident | (a) Type of
    Arrivals Only | Accommodation   [   ]   [   ]   [   ]
                       | Hotel/   Rented   Relative's/   Other
                       | Guest   Apt./   Friend's
                       | House   Cottage House
                       |
                       | (b) Purpose of Visit _____
                       |
                       | (c) Intended Length of Stay _____

10. For Residents of | (a) Purpose of Visit Abroad _____
    Barbados Only |
                       | (b) Length of Stay Abroad _____

11. Passport Number _____

12. Place and Date of Issue _____

                       _____
                                            Signature of Passenger

FOR OFFICIAL USE ONLY

Exercise   Consider the 'E/D form' shown above. It is a kind of form used to get
                    information from persons travelling abroad. Answer the following
                    questions:

1   Do you think that 'Ms' should be included? Give reasons.

2   Does 'Please Print' mean

    (i)   press hard

    (ii) write each letter separately

    (iii) use a typewriter?

3   What is the difference between 'Country of Birth' and 'Nationality'?

4   When you are sitting in the plane, which applies to you 7) or 8)?

5   What is the difference, if any, between 'Port of Disembarkation' and destination?

6   What does 8(b) mean?

7   What is the purpose of the questions in 9?

8   What does 12 mean? What is the purpose of this question?

Instructions and directions

Here is a shortlist of everyday things which involve following directions

- and instructions:

- using recipes in cooking

- taking medicine

- fixing appliances

- using equipment, motors, tools, appliances, computers

    assembling tools, toys, etc.

Most appliances which are bought in the store come with a booklet of instructions. Although the instructions are now always set out in the same way, they are usually in language simple enough for most non-technical people to understand. You can save yourself time, money and frustration if you read the instructions carefully before you attempt to use the appliance.

  Following instructions usually means going step by step. If you skip from place to place, you will miss essential details. Make sure you understand what each word means, because sometimes words are used with special meanings. Where arrows or other symbols are used instead of words or to accompany words, it is usually easier to follow the instructions.

BEFORE CALLING FOR SERVICE

CHECK THESE ITEMS	Re-orient antenna	Adjust color controls	Is it a color program?	Is TV power switch on?	Check for local interference	Adjust PICTURE control	Adjust BLACK LEVEL control	Is TV plugged in? Power in outlet?	Is antenna connected to terminals?	If outside antenna, check for broken wires	Try other Channel, if OK, possible station trouble
Picture OK. Sound poor	●				●						●
Sound OK. Picture poor	●				●	●	●		●	●	●
No picture or sound				●				●	●	●	●
Picture blurred	●									●	●
Ghosts in picture	●									●	●
Streaks or lines in picture	●				●					●	●
Weak picture	●						●		●	●	●
Bars on screen	●				●					●	
Poor color	●	●			●	●	●		●	●	●
No color	●	●	●						●	●	●
Picture distorted	●									●	●
Poor reception, some channels	●				●					●	●

Exercises

1   Convert the diagram above into a list of instructions using full sentences. Number each instruction.

2   Imagine you are a television repairman and you went to repair television sets at two homes. Using the diagram, write a report on the faults which you found and what action you took at each of the homes so that your supervisor can write up the bills for the owners.

3   Write instructions for any piece of equipment that you have or are familiar with either in a diagram form as here or in sentence form.

4   What is the advantage of the diagram form over the sentence form?

5   Why is it that all instructions cannot be set out in diagram form?

Panadol

Paracetamol Tablets Reg Trade Mark

Quickly Relieves Headaches and Pains
Reduces Fever

For the temporary relief of headache and
minor aches, pains associated with arthritis,
neuralgia, rheumatism and menstrual cramps.
Panadol reduces fever, helps relieve
discomforts of colds and flu. Gentle to the
stomach. Panadol may be used safely by
most persons with peptic ulcers when taken
as directed for recommended conditions.
Each tablet contains 500 mg paracetamol.
DOSAGE Adults – 1-2 tablets, three or four
times daily, not to exceed 8 tablets in 24
hours
Children 7-12 years – $\frac{1}{2}$ to 1 tablet three or
four times daily, not to exceed 4 tablets in 24
hours
For complete information see package insert.
In case of severe or recurrent pain or high or
continued fever, which may be indicative of
serious illness consult your physician.

DISPRIN ®

Disprin is taken in solution, so it is absorbed into the
bloodstream faster than solid tablets. It is ready to tackle
your pain fast.
For the relief of headache, toothache, neuralgia, period
pains, rheumatic pain, lumbago and sciatica. To relieve
the symptoms of influenza, feverishness, feverish colds
and ease sore throats.

DIRECTIONS: Dissolve in water before taking.

DOSE: Adults and children over 12 yrs. 1-3 tablets
(maximum 13 tablets in 24 hours).
Children 6-12 yrs. 1-2 tablets (maximum 8 tablets in 24
hours). The dose may be repeated after 4 hours but the
maximum dose in 24 hours must not be exceeded.
Children under 6 yrs. should be given Junior Disprin. If
Junior Disprin is not available the following fraction of
Disprin may be given:
Children: Age 4-6 yrs. $\frac{1}{2}$- 1 tablet
Maximum number of tablets in 24 hours 4
(under 4 years on doctor's advice only)

The dose may be repeated after 4 hours up to the
maximum daily dose. Do not continue dosage of
children for more than 3 days without consulting your
doctor. If symptoms persist consult your doctor.

**KEEP OUT OF REACH
OF CHILDREN**

| CONTAINS ASPIRIN | P |

EACH DISPRIN TABLET CONTAINS
300mg ASPIRIN BP

Exercises Read the instructions for Panadol and Disprin carefully and then answer
the following questions:

1   What is meant by 'in solution', what other instruction means the same
and what is the effect of taking Disprin this way?

2   List those ailments which each drug is said to relieve. What is the
difference between the two?

3   What active ingredients do the two drugs contain?

4   Why is it said that Panadol is safe for persons with ulcers and the same
claim is not made for Disprin?

5   Is Panadol the same thing as Disprin only with a different name?

6   In a family of two parents and four children the father, who suffers from

an ulcerated stomach, has influenza and complains that his joints are aching; the oldest son was playing football and complains of stiffness and muscular pain; the oldest daughter is having her monthly period; the last boy has a toothache and says that he cannot swallow tablets. The mother occasionally suffers with arthritis in her right hand but right now is feeling fine. Which of the two drugs and what dosage would you suggest each family member take?

Information in tables

You will already have met various kinds of tables. Every book contains a table of contents; every educational institution has a timetable; those of you who do mathematics will use books of mathematical tables.

A table can be simple, or it can have a great deal of information, using headings and sub-headings. A table presents information in columns (vertically) and in lines (horizontally). Both have to be read together to obtain information from the table. When there are many numbers and headings tables can be discouraging. You have to concentrate to follow the information line by line and column by column. The first important step in interpreting the information is to make sure you know what the headings mean.

The table overleaf presents statistics on the performance of students in CXC English in a particular year in various West Indian countries. Study it carefully and do not attempt the exercise until you are sure you understand the various entries.

Notes:

1   I, II, III, IV, V are the different grades that students obtained.

2   Regard I, II, III as passes and IV and V as failures.

3   The abbreviation 'No.' in the table means the number of students who got the grade indicated.

Exercises

1   Which territory had the largest number of students entering the exam? Which had the smallest?

2   Which territory had the highest percentage of students reaching Grade 1?

3   Name the territories where more students gained Grade III than Grade II.

4   Which territory did worst?

5   Are there territories which stand out for any reason whatsoever?

6   Say whether it is possible to tell whether the exam was hard/easy or whether the students that year were good/bad.

Summary Statistics for Subject Entry, Candidates Taking the Examination and Percentage Grade Distribution by Territory

GENERAL PROFICIENCY								
Territory	**Subject Entry**	**Cands. Writing Exam**		**I**	**II**	**III**	**IV**	**V**
Antigua	240	236	No. %	7 2.96	83 35.16	77 32.62	61 25.87	8 3.39
Barbados	2,060	2,044	No. %	348 17.02	695 34.00	548 26.82	436 21.33	17 0.83
Belize	508	489	No. %	49 10.02	187 38.24	132 26.99	117 23.92	4 0.83
B.V.I.	36	36	No. %	8 22.22	19 52.78	8 22.22	1 2.78	– –
Dominica	358	357	No. %	24 6.72	109 30.53	107 29.98	114 31.93	3 0.84
Grenada	307	305	No. %	21 6.89	97 31.80	90 29.51	90 29.51	7 2.29
Guyana	3,433	3,377	No. %	123 3.64	525 15.54	685 20.28	1,604 47.49	440 13.05
Jamaica	11,562	11,387	No. %	771 6.77	3,073 26.98	3,171 27.84	3,881 34.08	491 4.33
Montserrat	46	46	No. %	9 19.56	27 58.69	9 19.56	1 2.19	– –
St. Kitts	207	207	No. %	33 15.94	78 37.68	59 28.50	34 16.44	3 1.44
St. Lucia	555	548	No. %	18 8.75	185 33.75	166 30.29	140 25.54	9 1.67
St. Vincent	375	375	No. %	29 7.73	123 32.80	81 21.60	133 35.47	9 2.40
Trinidad & Tobago	17,387	15,776	No. %	1,546 9.79	3,798 24.09	3,762 23.84	5,487 34.79	1,183 7.49
Anguilla	19	19	No. %	5 26.31	6 31.57	7 36.84	1 5.28	– –
Turks & Caicos Is.	14	14	No. %	–	5 35.75	6 42.85	2 14.28	1 7.14

Information in maps and diagrams

Almost everyone knows what a map is and will have used one at one time or another. However, very few people actually use the *key* that is provided with most maps. Here is an example of a map key.

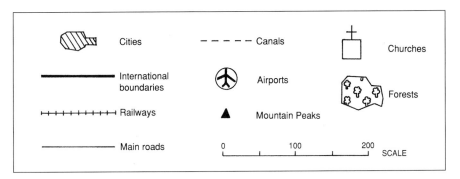

Use the map key to explain in two paragraphs in your own words what information this map provides. Describe/explain the symbols and say what they represent.

The map below shows where agricultural products come from in the Caribbean. Look at the key to make sure which drawing represents which item.

Exercise   Using the map, construct a table showing the agricultural products of the different countries of the Caribbean.

The following map shows the city of Charlestown. Study it carefully.

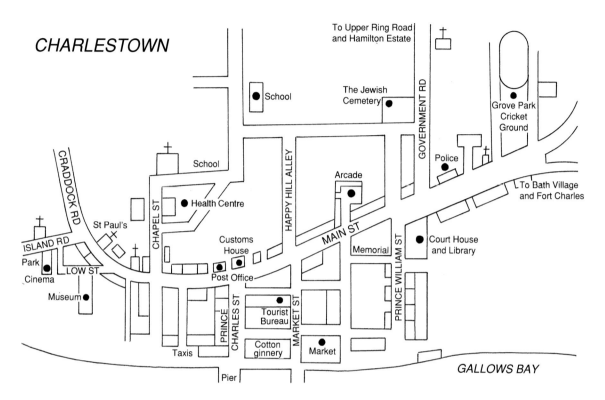

Exercises   1   Imagine that you are an employee at the Tourist Bureau on Market Street and four different tourists come into the Bureau to you to get directions to specific places in Charlestown. Using only the information on the map and only the streets with names on the map, say exactly how you would direct the tourists to

(i)   the museum   (ii) the cricket ground

(iii) the Jewish cemetery   (iv) the health centre

Remember that the tourists intend to walk and so should be told what they will pass en route.

2   If you came into Charlestown by boat and had to go to the Customs House, what street would you travel on?

3   If you were coming from the direction of Upper Ring Road and you were going to the cinema, what streets would you pass

(i)   on your right hand side? (ii) on your left hand side?

4   How many churches are identified on the map?

A plan is a special kind of map usually covering a small area. Plans for proposed new buildings, especially houses, occur quite normally in the newspaper. Look at the plan of a house below.

Exercise

Imagine that a relative or friend asked you to explain the plan in detail. Use the key provided and in essay form explain clearly and concisely the features (i.e. parts and contents) of the proposed house.

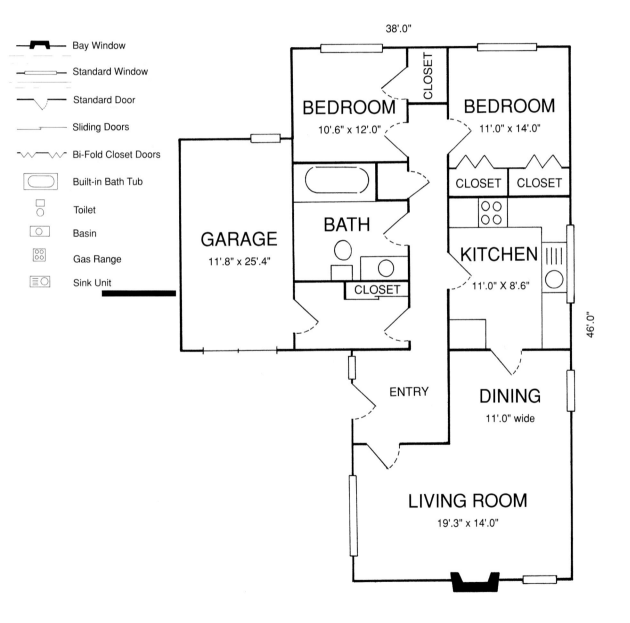

Section B Language work

Vocabulary

Descriptive phrases

In giving information you should be able to translate what you observe into writing and, just as important, you should have in mind categories and labels to help you to observe in full and in detail.

Note the following lists for describing objects and persons, with examples of descriptive words:

Objects

shape:	round, flat, irregular
size:	large, narrow, short
shade:	dark, dull, dazzling
substance:	wood, glass, stone
pattern:	striped, spotted, spattered, blotched
position:	upright, bent, horizontal, suspended
texture:	smooth, shiny, hard, moist, sticky

Persons

height:	tall, average, short, dwarf-like
weight:	average, heavy, light
build:	skinny, well-built, stout, lanky, slim
racial features:	black, brown-skinned, dark-haired
age:	young, teenaged, elder, aged
demeanour:	haughty, shifty, confident, alert
dress:	shabby, sharp, conservative, fashionable
speech:	slurred, foreign, halting

Descriptive words should be used in combination with the object or person you are describing. When you use one or more than one descriptive word (adjective) plus a noun, the reader immediately gets a better picture of what you are describing and as a result your language and description will seem more mature. As in all other things, combinations should not be too elaborate or overused.

Exercises

Your house has been broken into and a number of items stolen.

1   Write out for the police a description of the items stolen.

2   Describe for the police a suspicious character who was lurking in the neighbourhood recently.

Sentence composition

Instruction and explanation

Look at the differences in the following:

Instruction	*Explanation*
Put some seeds in a cup.	Some seeds were put in a cup.
Boil the potatoes first.	The potatoes were boiled first.
Check the gas.	The gas was checked by the attendant.
Light the match before you turn on the gas.	The match was lit before the gas was turned on.

Exercises

Below there are ten verbs given as five pairs.

1   Use each pair of verbs in a sentence to give an explanation, making the first verb positive and the second negative.

2   Convert each sentence into one giving instructions.

Example: move, spill

a) The water was moved in the basin without it being spilled.

b) Move the water in the basin, but don't spill it.

sink	broadcast
burst	spoil
swell	draw
lose	hang
steal	recover

Writing Summaries

Objectives

This unit will help you to:

✓ write summaries of various kinds of writing
✓ choose the best summary when presented with several
✓ learn how to understand a passage by looking at the way common words are used

**Section A
Guidance**

In writing it is often a great advantage to be able to present your ideas, comments, answers and arguments precisely and in as short a space as possible, without leaving out important points. For example, a newspaper reporter has to be able to summarise; a movie or book critic has to explain the movie/book and comment on it in a few hundred words; an adviser to a minister, manager or board has to present the pros and cons clearly and concisely so that decisions can be made in good time. It is an important skill therefore to be able to reduce statements and arguments to the 'bones' and to present these 'bones' in as appealing a manner as possible. In order to do this you need to use sentences which are tightly constructed and words that are precise, with a simple coherent movement from one sentence to the next.

How to write a summary of a passage

1 Read the passage.

2 Read it again and note down the main points. Distinguish between points and examples used to explain points: to do this look out for words like 'for example', 'for instance'; look out for parts of sentences beginning with 'who', 'which', 'where'. These words indicate examples or details.

3 Read it again, check your notes and amend where necessary.

4 Put aside the passage and write a first draft of the summary using your notes:

• Do not change or add anything to suit your own point of view.

• Do not exaggerate one way or the other. You should be able to summarise a position without distortion, whether you agree with it or not.

5 Read the passage again and then put it aside.

6 Edit your draft:

• Change words to capture the meaning of the passage.

- Connect up your sentences to make them run smoothly by using words like however, since, therefore, consequently.

- Remove ungrammatical and awkward parts.

- The summary must read like a passage, not like notes of a passage.

7   Do not try to do a summary by merely striking out words or sentences from the original. Writing a summary is not necessarily an exercise in reducing long-winded phrases and jargon to shorter, simpler ones. You should use your own words as far as possible.

Types of summary

Summaries must differ according to the types of writing involved and the substance of the writing. Passages with descriptions require a different kind of summary from those with arguments. For instance, a passage written in the jargon of the subject normally requires simplification to make the summary intelligible. Summaries of emotive writing must differ in tone and word choice from summaries of scientific objective writing.

A passage may contain one main point stated briefly with illustrations/ explanations of this point, or a passage may contain several main points. In the former case, depending on the length specified for the summary, you may summarise just by giving the main point, or you may give the main point together with a summary of the illustrations/explanations. In the latter case, you have only to give a summary of the main points.

It is therefore important to decide on the type of writing the passage presents before you attempt any summary.

Passage 1

In Jamaica and the Windward Islands, where the availability of large tracts of unused land for peasant activity frequently resulted in the withdrawal of labourers from the estates, governments were concerned that emigration would further reduce the islands' agricultural labour force. Indeed, in Jamaica this concern was expressed by Governor Norman during the 1880s, and by Governors Olivier and Swettenham between 1904 and 1906. It was partly responsible for the lukewarmness with which administrators, planters and commercial groups in the Windward Islands regarded the ICC's recruiting agents, and emigration to Panama after 1905. On the other hand, in Barbados and St Kitts, where plantation labourers were plentiful, and especially in the former island, where emigration was regarded as a means of reducing a high population density, governments did not complain of, nor attempt to restrict emigration on account of labour shortages until 1911. By this time, the movement to Panama would have been considerably less than in former years.

Analysis of passage 1

Finding the main points

Read the whole of passage 1 and then read the underlined parts again. You will see that the underlined parts are the two main points in the paragraph.

The clauses that begin 'where ...' are explaining by giving information:

- 'where the availability ... from the estates'
- 'where plantation labourers ..., where emigration ... density'

The sentence 'Indeed, in Jamaica ... and 1906' is also explaining by giving information, specifically about Jamaica.

   In the passage, therefore, the author (and this is what authors generally do) makes a point, then explains it, makes another and again explains it.

   In a summary your task is to capture the main point or points without expansion. However, you cannot simply rewrite the main point in the exact words of the author. You have to make it understandable. In addition, in this paragraph there is a contrast between Jamaica and the Windwards on the one hand and Barbados and St Kitts on the other. Your summary should maintain that contrast.

Exercise

Write a summary of the paragraph in one sentence.

Passage 2

Taking time to prepare a budget allows the family to make choices which will benefit every member. It helps the family anticipate future financial commitments (whether in a week, a number of months or a year) ahead of time and plan to meet these commitments. Food, clothing, housing, education, recreation, old age and security must be budgeted for, also any emergencies which might occur. Budgeting also allows the family to contemplate different spending alternatives clearly, assess their relative value and make wise decisions.

   Budgeting concerns every member of the family. Everyone should take part. Children should be exposed to the concept of budgeting early so that they will be prepared to cope independently with situations, such as being away from home and living on an income of their own. Knowing how to budget and then establishing the right pattern of money management will enable them to make ends meet.

   People tend to spend their money in ways which give them the greatest satisfaction. Some have smaller incomes than others and spend most of their income on food, the most important item of expenditure. If a certain level of food consumption is to be maintained, less money will be left for other needs, especially when prices are high.

Far too often consumers are tempted into spending more than is really necessary. Catchy advertising, attractive store displays and fancy packaging are some of the inducements which tempt us into parting with our hard-earned dollars and cents.

Analysis of passage 2

Passage 1 was written by a historian, but passage 2 is by a teacher of home economics. The intentions and styles of the two are different. In passage 1 the writer is explaining the past, whereas in passage 2 the writer is advising about the future. In writing a summary of passage 2, therefore, you should bear in mind the objective of the writer and try to preserve it – your summary should give advice clearly but without expansion and details.

In passage 2 the paragraphs are short and every paragraph starts off with a piece of advice. In paragraphs one and two the idea in the first sentence in each case is developed in the rest of the paragraph. However, in paragraph three there are two ideas – people's preferences and the part of the budget spent on food.

Exercise

Write a summary of the passage by joining the underlined parts to form two smooth, coherent sentences. You may rearrange the sentences if you wish.

Passage 3

Despite all the difficulties of creating savings for investment, the mistakes made in economic policy, and the distortions that accompanied the whole process of development, the economy has nevertheless made satisfactory progress in the last few decades. During the period from 1955 to 1975 for instance, the real product grew at an average annual rate of slightly under 8%, corresponding to an increase of about 5.0% per capita.

In the years following the Second World War, government and private enterprise found the investment needed for the cumulative raising of the real product so as to keep pace with the demographic increase, without making more demands on the population than they could bear. In general, the objects were attained, though already by the first half of the decade from 1960 to 1970 a distinct recession was beginning to be felt as a result of the distortions occurring in the process and the lack of effective corrective measures.

Analysis of passage 3

Passage 3 was written by an economist and such passages usually contain jargon which requires interpretation. The author's concern is the growth of 'the real product'. Even if you don't understand the precise meaning of this term, you should be able to gain some understanding of it from reading the passage as a whole. In other words, you do not need to understand the term like an economist to be able to do a summary of the passage.

The author is assessing the performance of the economy of the country over the last few decades. The first underlined sentence is an over-all assessment. He then breaks down the 'last few decades' into 'the period 1955 to 1975', 'the years following the Second World War' (i.e. 1945 onward) and 'the first half of the decade from 1960 to 1970'. Your summary does not have to reflect the details of these periods except that it has to mention what is in the second underlined part, since this is a new point which because of the wording ('was beginning to be felt') seems to be pointing to something later.

Exercise

Write a summary of the passage by joining the underlined parts. Make the second part subordinate to the first. Produce a smooth coherent sentence. You may change or substitute words.

Passage 4

It must be clearly understood that man is only beginning to unravel some of the mysteries involved in the functioning of the brain. There   is much that we do not know; for example, no one knows where the seats of memory and will power are located. Experimenters do not simply open the skull of a living human being and run some tests; data must be accumulated from patients with brain lesions (diseased areas) and trauma (wounds), and these data must be evaluated over periods of years. When an individual must have a portion of his brain exposed during surgery, he is often conscious (the brain itself is insensitive to pain), so portions of the brain may be lightly stimulated and the patient asked to describe any sensations he may experience. Also, motor reactions (movements) are noted. <u>These data together with that accumulated from animal experimentation and detailed microscopic examination, constitute man's knowledge of his brain.</u> It should also be pointed out that the brain and the 'mind' are not synonymous. The brain is a dissectible organ; but the mind is an abstraction, referrring to mental activity that takes place in the physical organ, the brain.

Analysis of passage 4

Passage 4 is scientific in that it deals with a part of the human body, but there is not much scientific jargon. The passage is not a description, it is an assessment of man's knowledge of the brain, pointing out

• what is known

• what is not known

• reasons for knowing and not knowing

The last point made in the passage about the difference between the brain and the mind is not a main point here; it is merely a clarification to make sure that the reader is clear that the author is dealing with the brain and not the mind. It need not be included in a summary. A summary of this passage should reflect the author's over-all assessment of what is known, what is not known and the reasons.

Exercise

Write a summary of the passage in three sentences. Reword the points in the underlined sentence and use it as your main sentence.

Passage 5

In this <u>UNESCO has a ready-made task</u> to assist in ridding the Caribbean region of an overbearing Eurocentric cultural domination, by <u>decentralising its own activities</u> and transforming Paris, its present headquarters, into just one of many centres in the diverse world it is supposed to serve. The world organisation also needs to discredit any tradition of thought which views 'culture' as an elitist expression by a privileged few within nations and internationally. There were, indeed, more than glimpses of this lingering perception in the presentations of some delegations as they lauded the civilising power of the Great Tradition of metropolitan culture. <u>UNESCO and the OAS could well encourage and promote the view of culture as a dynamic cyclical process of growth in human development</u> – a process in which the rich textured experience of the mass of the people forms the source of energy for cultural expressions in both classic and popular modes, making cultural products the result of organic interaction between all classes and manner of people. <u>For Latin American–Caribbean co-operation in the field of culture depends firstly on the disappearance of colonial notions</u> which transform native people into anthropological specimens to be civilised into a master culture <u>and, secondly, on the recognition that there is a common meeting ground in the shared experience of a creolisation process.</u> In fact, UNESCO and the OAS will have to be prepared to address themselves increasingly and specifically to the processes of cultural development rather than to the products so as to (i) facilitate the work they do in areas of intra-regional and inter-national cultural co-operation and exchange and (ii) avoid the perpetuation of one unfortunate aspect of Caribbean experience whereby things metropolitan are placed high in some hierarchy of cultural values while things produced by the colonised and formerly colonised peoples are dismissed as subordinate. <u>A new international cultural order is no less needed than a new international economic order.</u>

Analysis of passage 5

The parts underlined in the paragraph are the main points. One of the difficulties in identifying the main points in this passage is that the reader tends to be overly influenced by the negative language (e.g. ridding, discredit, disappearance, unfortunate, dismissed) which relates to only one of the author's two recommendations and which almost overshadows the author's positive definition of culture. A summary has to reflect the author's definition of culture and his two recommendations on how this new cultural development should be achieved in the Caribbean.

Exercise

Write a summary of the passage using the underlined sections.

Passage 6

<u>Fears for the extinction of the dialect in East Anglia, as in other parts of England, are not, of course, new.</u> Towards the end of the nineteenth century when Joseph Wright was busy compiling his massive, six volume English Dialect Dictionary for the whole nation because he felt time was running out, the Eastern Daily Press newspaper in Norwich which has always been a focus for the dialect's preservation, published a book of readers' letters on the subject under the title *Broad Norfolk*. In its preface the editor of the paper expressed his apprehension that this would probably be a final salute to a way of speaking that was doomed to die out in the next generation. But that was in 1893, and fifty years later in 1949 the same newspaper found itself publishing a similar book under the same title as a result of a phenomenal surge of correspondence from readers written in and about the allegedly moribund dialect that was sparked off by an innocent enquiry about local names for British birds.

Even today there is something inexplicable about the way in which the dialect is surviving. In a curious way it could even be said to be flourishing because the population changes and the growing influence of the mass media that have contributed towards the decline of dialect are now paradoxically fostering a revival of interest in it. Television and radio programmes dealing with the subject are enormously popular in East Anglia. One parson in the county has become famous for his television broadcasting of stories from the Bible 'translated' into broad Norfolk, and books written around the nostalgia and humour of the dialect are finding rapidly increasing markets – not least among those people new to the region who presumably wish to increase their sense of identity and belonging.

Analysis of passage 6

In passage 6 there is a single main theme followed by three illustrations of it. The main theme is partially expressed in the underlined sentence; it can be stated simply as 'threats to the extinction of dialect cause its revival'. To illustrate this point the author then cites three time periods when this happened:

- 'Towards the end of the nineteenth century'

- 'Fifty years later in 1949'

- 'Even today'

Since the passage is taken up with the illustrations of the main theme, a summary of the passage can be very short, simply stating the main theme, or, if longer, it would have to give the main theme together with a short reference to each of the three illustrations.

Exercise

Write a summary of the passage in not more than 70 words.

Choosing the best summary

You may be presented with three or four different summaries of a passage and asked to choose the best one. To do this, you need to be able to spot the weaknesses of some summaries. For instance, a summary may

- leave out important points

- add points which are not there

- misinterpret the original or say the complete opposite

- be accurate, but use a style different from the original

Here are some pointers to follow:

- Read the passage twice before you do anything else.

- Read each summary.

- Immediately eliminate any summary which makes a new point – one that is not in or implied in the original.

- Do not choose or eliminate any summary because of its length.

- If you are left with two summaries which seem close, concentrate on picking up slight changes in emphasis or point of view from the original. See if one passage has a greater number of points or a more comprehensive phrasing than the other.

<table>
<tr><td>

**Section B
Language
work**

</td></tr>
</table>

Vocabulary

How to understand the meaning of a passage

When working on a summary writing, it obviously helps if you understand the meaning of most of the words in the passage. However, accurate understanding very often results from carefully looking at the sentence structure and paying attention to very familiar and frequently occurring words and phrases.

Common words which help you to understand a passage:

- listing words

- cause and effect words

- explanatory words

- contrast words

Listing words

The following words help you to follow the development of ideas in a passage. They are words which you yourself should get accustomed to using in presenting ideas in an orderly fashion.

Listing signals

Adverbs	Verbs
first	begin/start
second/next	continue/become
third/then	remain/develop
last/finally	end/finish/culminate

You may find yourself using the words above in short, simple sentences. If you want to make longer sentences of two or more clauses, use the following:

before; until; when; while; as soon as; after; having done ..., she ...

Exercise

Change one of the verbs to 'Having ... '; put the having clause last. E.g.:

He ran away. He did not know what happened.

He did not know what happened, having run away.

1   The manager lost the match. He had to resign.

2   The woman reached the age of sixty. She retired.

3   The pupil had too many mistakes in his essay. He had to rewrite it.

4   Baba was found guilty of murder. He was sentenced to hang

5   The champion was floored twice. He came back to win the fight.

Cause and effect words

It is fairly easy to understand cause and effect words like 'so','since', 'because'. E.g.

> He broke his toe because he kicked the tyre so hard.

> He kicked the tyre so hard that he broke his toe.

However, there are other words which are very often treated by readers as if they do not have a precise meaning. At the beginning of a sentence words like 'therefore', 'consequently', 'hence' have the same kind of meaning as 'so', 'since' and 'because' used in the middle of a sentence. The difference is that words like 'therefore' are used to introduce a conclusion after a number of statements have been made.

Explanatory words

Many students who have difficulty distinguishing between the main point and an example given to illustrate or explain a point may simply be disregarding words/phrases such as 'for example', 'namely', 'viz', 'for instance'. What causes the reader to ignore these words is that the example is often more appealing, easier to understand and takes up more of the paragraph than the point which the author is making.

Contrast words

In presenting an argument an author may give more than one viewpoint or may present differing facts. In order to highlight such differences, specific words can be used. E.g.

> Last year was a total disaster, <u>but</u> this year is completely different.

> <u>Whereas / While</u> last year was a total disaster, this year is completely different.

> <u>In contrast to / Unlike</u> last year, which was a total disaster, this year ...

Last year was a total disaster. <u>However / In contrast / On the other hand</u>, this year ...

Over a long argument, an author will try to vary the use of these contrast words as well as the structure of the words in which they occur.

Assignment

Look at newspaper articles for examples of all the above categories of words. Highlight the places where they occur and bring the articles into class for discussion with other students.

Understanding the Spoken Language

Objectives

This unit will help you to:

✓ appreciate how speech is made up
✓ understand the importance of speech in today's world
✓ write reported speech correctly
✓ see how the pronunciation of some words changes when they change their form
✓ deal with words which change their meaning when they split into two
✓ practise spelling some difficult words

**Section A
Guidance**

How speech is made up

Speech is so natural that you do not normally pay any attention to the complexity of it. In addition to the individual sounds in words (i.e. the consonants and vowels), speech has intonation (i.e. the rises and falls of the voice as the speaker goes along) as well as stress (i.e. words or parts of words pronounced with more force than others). Speech also has pauses (i.e. the stops and starts accompanied by *uh's* and *ah's* made while the speaker is thinking) and what are called 'mazes' (i.e. changes in thought and sentence structure before the sentence is finished).

All speech is produced with a certain tone of voice which can be changed at will and which shows the attitude of the speaker. Of course all speakers have an 'accent', but an individual can only hear someone else's 'accent' and not his/her own. In face to face communication speech is accompanied by body language (i.e. movement of parts of the face, the head, the hands, the arms, the shoulders and the positioning of the body as a whole), which is so much a part of communication that when some people are restricted from using their hands and shoulders they have great problems getting over what they want to say.

The importance of speech in today's world

Although speaking has always been more important for human beings than any other means of communicating, it was much less influential before amplified sound, radio, television and recording became widespread. In the olden days a speaker could be heard only by those close enough to hear, that is, at most by a few thousand people and only while actually speaking. Nowadays a speech can be heard by millions of people while the speaker is actually speaking or at any time afterwards.

So, because a speaker's voice and words can now reach a limitless number of people, speech has been developed in sophisticated ways in order to inform people of news and to persuade people in business, politics and religion.

Graduates look good, but are they?

JOB-HUNTING graduates write good letters and look good when they appear for interviews but do not know how to handle the interview, have difficulties speaking English and are unfamiliar with modern office machines, a **Sunday Gleaner** survey showed.

Personnel managers said the interview is what determines whether the school leaver lands the job s/he is going after or whether s/he has to go further afield.

Two teenagers just leaving high school apply for a position in a bank. Both have exactly the same qualifications, and the same lack of experience. Both are above average intelligence. One gets the job as a bank teller, or whatever other job being offered, the other does not. Why?

'One is more positive, one projects himself more than others,' says Patricia Palmer, personnel manager of Life of Jamaica.

Company representatives interviewed by the **Sunday Gleaner** said that in most cases letters of application by school leavers, are well written. There are some recurring errors, Elaine Robinson personnel

manager of Price Waterhouse says.

'I find the applications look very good,' says an officer of Grace Kennedy and Company Limited. 'They give a good impression, but when they (applicants) come in they are not as impressive as the letters they write.'

School leavers seem either not to know or not to understand that they must sell themselves, when they attend an interview. 'When they come to be interviewed we wish they came knowing what to ask, being more conversational,' Mrs Robinson says. 'It's a pleasure to interview someone who talks.'

People recruiting school leavers say they look closely at the applicant's ability to succeed in the profession they are entering. They employ people whom they feel will be able to cope with the type of work the company offers. They look at the aptitude of the applicants, their dress, deportment, speech, mannerisms, and assess their general knowledge and knowledge of current affairs.

Most companies, contacted by the **Sunday Gleaner** say they want ambitious, independent and hard-working people willing to learn and anxious to get ahead and able to get on with others.

The language of the school leavers is another problem. Many applicants attend the interview with good grades in English Language but they cannot write or speak it. Good interpersonal relationships and the ability to speak English are key features, especially for persons who deal with the public, the Grace Kennedy spokesman says.

In addition, many applicants do not possess the required qualifications and skills to be placed in the job they are seeking. Some do not have four or five passes in G.C.E. 'O' level or the CXC examinations. And the typing is not 'too hot', companies getting applications say.

Inept

Most companies say they have a hard time finding secretaries. The secretaries often fail the aptitude test, find difficulty in writing certain types of letters and are not accustomed to using the electric typewriter. One of the drawbacks is the general lack of equipment in the school system. Many of the students are not exposed to the things taken for granted in the work place – telephones, calculators, electric typewriters and computers.

Dressing is not such a serious problem for the high school leaver seeking a job. Most of them try to dress appropriately but some turn up in jeans and T shirts. And some come with all kinds of 'fandangles'. 'They just seem too laid back and casual', Corina Meeks of Creative Projects says.

Men seem to have a harder time in interviews, says Arlene Irons, staff manager of National Commercial Bank.

'No matter how well qualified they are, they are not able to conduct themselves as well through an interview.' This is somewhat unfortunate, as the bank needs a better mixture of men and women, Mrs Irons says. But employment must be based on the results of the interview. One of the biggest mistakes is to employ someone out of sympathy, Mrs Irons says. That person will turn around to haunt you.

Little things count

'The market is very competitive and we need young energetic, bright, confident people,' says Mr Harold Mignott, personnel manager of Seprod Ltd.

In order to gain employment, school leavers must try to understand as early as possible that they need to sell themselves in the job interview, managers say.

School leavers who have taken off their graduation gowns and the nice dress worn to the ceremony must learn the 'little things' that are important if they manage to get to the door for an interview:

• Sit properly without slumping.

• Never drop your guard, that is do not get overly friendly with your interviewer.

• Look at the interviewer. It is an indication that you are not the right person if you cannot look the interviewer in the face.

The bottom line is 'if you don't sell yourself, nobody will sell it for you'.

Questions

1   In the previous passage identify two comments made by employers which show the importance of speech in interviews.

2   What do employers look for in prospective employees?

3   What is meant by the phrases 'project yourself' and 'sell yourself'? Say exactly how you would do this in an interview.

4   How important is the interview in getting a job? Give reasons for your answer.

5   Identify the reasons given why some applicants are unsuccessful in getting jobs.

6   What is the one specific failing for which the school system is blamed?

7   What, if any, is the difference between male and female school-leavers in their performance in interviews?

8   In two paragraphs give your reactions to the statements made in the passage, making sure to point out what you think is the best and fairest way to select someone for a job.

The following article was written by Nicholas Bagnall and appeared in a British newspaper in 1987.

Nicholas Bagnall on a controversial oral exam in English
Can the spoken word be tested fairly?

THE WORD 'oracy' has not long been in the dictionaries, but by next year thousands of school-children will know what it means, since it will be a compulsory element of the GCSE English examination.

The Government's national criteria for the GCSE, so often rather vague and unhelpful, are clear on this point. 'The assessment objectives,' says the English section in its ugly prose, 'must provide opportunities for candidates to demonstrate their ability to ... communicate effectively in spoken English.'

Unfortunately the business of testing the spoken word is full of hazards. So until assessment techniques can be made reliable candidates will get a double certificate: a main grade, and a separate one for oracy. But everyone will need at least Grade 5 in it to pass the exam as a whole.

An example of the hazards: examiners who mark written scripts do their best not to be influenced by handwriting, though they may subtract marks for bad 'presentation' and spelling. How very much harder to ignore their oral equivalents: not only the examinees' accents, but also their facial expressions and, indeed, their whole body language.

Tapes might seem the answer, but in practice they can take up an unmanageable amount of time. Perversely, too, they may do candidates less than justice because, unless they are transcribed and edited so as to cut out the hesitations, false starts, ellipses and repetitions we all use

when we are talking, they can make even a very intelligent speaker sound inarticulate; this is as true of ex-President Nixon as it is of a bright fifth-former. But a transcription will not do either, since we bring to it the expectations of a reader rather than a listener, thus presumably defeating the object.

Just as tricky is the problem of how to set up an oral exam in the first place. CSE English had an oral element, though not a compulsory one. Pupils were required to read from a text or to conduct among themselves a debate on some issue of the day in the inhibiting presence of the examiner. Or it might be done by formal talks or interviews.

Pupils must have a reason for spouting

The GCSE examiners will try to order things better. One idea is to get away from those 'random exchanges of views' of the sort which one hears in the BBC's *Stop the Week*. There must be a *purpose*, say the National criteria. To avoid the artificiality of a set debate, pupils must be given a feeling that they have a reason for spouting, apart, of course, from the mere desire for marks.

But the examiners must also be clear what *their* purpose is. 'There is likely to be uncertainty,' said a guide for teachers put out last year by the Secondary Examinations Council, 'over what to assess, and how.' Those last two words are not a colloquialism, though they might well have been.

A syllabus devised last year by the Midland Examining Group carried a seven-point list of things for which

candidates would be awarded marks in group discussions. They included: organisation of ideas, clarity of delivery, directness of communication, giving convincing expression to thoughts and feelings, ability to develop ideas and so on.

How are all these qualities to be identified and evaluated? The Government's Assessment of Performance Unit has been trying out various techniques, as part of its Language Monitoring Project, for judging oracy. The APU points out that not all of the exercises it has used for these dummy runs would be right for the national exam. In some the pupil was encouraged to talk about 'the most interesting thing learned recently,' or to describe a complicated bridge structure, or an experiment he or she had just done, or to explain, say, how a spider makes her web. Assessors are advised not to prompt the pupil.

In other exercises, two or more pupils were asked to imagine they were in different jobs and to discuss which was the most valuable: a somewhat 'artificial' set-up. In another, two pupils were each given a map, one of which was out of date, and the pupil with the up-to-date map was asked to give directions, as though on the telephone, to the other.

Some of the transcribed results have been published and in many of them it seems clear that what is being tested is imagination and intelligence rather than a detachable quality called 'oracy'. The assessment routines suggested are remarkably cumbersome. Nevertheless, the APU claims 'a significant advance in the testing of spoken language'. Meanwhile, the School Curriculum

Development Committee is about to launch a monster project in schools; it will cost £1.5m and take six years.

The part played by speech in learning

Its object is not only to find ways of making children talk better, and of testing them at it, but also to 'raise the status of talk in the classroom for pupils of all ages', and 'enhance the role of speech in the learning process', in the words of Keith Kirby, the Committee's energetic principal professional officer.

A considered attack on the whole concept appeared at the beginning of this year in the Salisbury Review, the Tory quarterly. Its author, Jonathan Worthen, called the oral element in the GCSE 'particularly meretricious' and 'opposed to real learning'. Arguing that 'good spoken English results from good teaching based on written English', he declared: 'The aim of the GCSE is in fact to breed out traditional literary study by surrounding it by a mishmash of other ways of responding to literature,' and he feared for 'the traditional discursive essay'.

Keith Kirby at the SCDC, and the oracy project's director, John Johnson, indignantly defend their position, pointing to the part speech has always played in teaching, from Socrates' time, through the medieval schools, down to the Oxford tutorial. 'What are undergraduates' supervisions and seminars if not a verbal interchange?' Mr Johnson said.

Both deny that oral learning need temper the wind to weaker pupils. Mr Kirby said: 'I see talking and writing having similar aims. We tend to use writing for things we already know but speech can often be a more effective way of learning. The APU found that pupils could solve problems in science by talking together which baffled them when they tackled them alone.

'Most people would agree that their ability to talk has been far more closely connected with their success in life than writing has. The schools reverse this. We're trying to get rid of the idea that talk isn't work.'

The questions remain. How to grade spoken performance fairly? How to make sure that talking in class does not slide into idle chatter, but as Mr Kirby and Mr Johnson would like, is truly an extension of the curriculum? And that those qualities listed by the Midland Examining Group are not examined *in vacuo?*

'We don't know the answers,' said Mr Kirby. It seems a pity that the project was not mounted earlier. And how.

Questions

1 What is 'oracy'?

2 What reasons are given for the introduction of an oral examination in English?

3 The article deals with many problems involved in the testing of the spoken word. What are the different types of problems identified?

4 What, according to the article, is Jonathan Worthen's view of the project to test oracy? (Use your own words.)

5 What, according to the article, is Kirby and Johnson's reply to Worthen? (Use your own words.)

6 Do you think that 'ability to talk has been far more closely connected with ... success in life than writing has'? Give reasons for your opinion.

Assignment

Write an essay of 300 words arguing for or against the introduction of an oral exam in English by CXC.

Section B
Language
work

Sentence composition

Reported speech

You listen to a friend of yours recite a number of things that she has done and is doing, but you know that she is not doing the things herself.

> 'I cut my hair, I have fixed my car and I have built a new house. Right now I am putting in a new carpet and I am decorating the living room. I have already put up burglar bars and curtains at all the windows. I have not installed any glass doors because I do not like them. I am painting the outside of the house and cleaning up the yard. I hope to finish everything by the end of next month. I will move in my things by truck.'

Rewrite what she said according to what you think really happened, using the following pattern:

> My friend told me that she had her hair cut, she has had her car fixed ...(continue)

Vocabulary

Changes in pronunciation

In Standard English some words change their pronunciation, not their spelling, according to whether they are nouns or verbs. Because such changes are not always reflected in everyday West Indian speech, it is good to become familiar with them.

When these words change from nouns to verbs the stress is changed from the first syllable to the last:

conduct	rebel	progress
conflict	incense	record
convert	object	subject
convict	present	torment
produce	content	permit
protest	contest	suspect
contrast		

Exercise

Choose six of the above words. Use each of them in two sentences, as a noun in the first, as a verb in the second. Read the sentences out loud to a friend.

Punctuation

Joining and splitting of words

Whereas some words may be written as one word or two words without any difference in meaning or grammar (e.g. taperecorder/tape recorder; folktale/folk tale), others have a clear difference when written as one in contrast to when written as two. E.g.

every body	everybody (pronoun)	
every day	everyday (adjective)	
may be	maybe (adverb)	
some time	sometime (adjective)	sometimes (adverb)
all together	altogether	
any way	anyway (adverb)	
all right	alright	

Examples:

1   There were six bodies lying on the grass and every body was covered with blood.

2   That is an everyday occurrence, but that doesn't mean that it has to happen every day.

3   Altogether there were fifty children and they went to the show all together.

4   'Maybe he's at school,' I said, 'but then again he may be at home by now.'

5   Your sometime friend comes to look for you sometimes.

Note:

• 'All right' and 'alright' have the same meaning, but alright is not regarded as suitable for formal writing.

• The words 'cannot' and 'everywhere' should always be written as one word in each case.

Exercise

Write pairs of sentences showing the different meanings of:

any way/anyway

may be/maybe

every body/everybody

Spelling

Exercise

Indicate the correct spelling of the following by identifying the appropriate letter A, B or C.

	A	B	C
1	nescessary	necessary	neccessary
2	buisness	business	bussiness
3	pyschology	pyscholagy	psychology
4	humorous	humourous	humourus
5	seize	sieze	sieize
6	precede	preceede	preceed
7	priviledge	privilege	privalege
8	consientious	conscientious	concientious
9	comparitive	comparitave	comparative
10	embarass	embarrass	embarras
11	skillful	skilful	skilfull
12	separate	seperate	seperrate
13	surprise	supprise	suprise
14	acquaintance	aquaintence	aquaintance
15	ocassion	occasion	ocasion
16	paralel	parrallel	parallel
17	develop	develope	devellop
18	hypotenuise	hypotanuse	hypotenuse
19	negligiblen	negligeable	negligable
20	accommodation	acommodation	accomodation
21	undoubtably	undoubtedly	undoutedly
22	secetary	secretery	secretary
23	supercede	superceed	supersede
24	occurance	occurrence	occurence
25	beneficial	benefitial	benificial

The Spoken Language in the West Indies

Objectives

This unit will help you to:

✓ convert patois into Standard English
✓ understand what is meant by colloquial language
✓ recognise slang words and expressions
✓ appreciate that some words are stressed for emphasis in speech
✓ improve your punctuation
✓ correct spelling errors by knowing about homophones

The story of patois

The word 'patois' has two meanings in the West Indies. In Jamaica, mostly, people use it to mean the same thing as 'the dialect'. In most of the other territories it is used to refer to the language spoken by most St Lucians and Dominicans.

Patois, in the latter sense, has the same early history as West Indian English (see Unit 6) except that instead of the slaves learning English from English speakers they were learning French from French speakers. Patois speakers in St Lucia, Dominica, Martinique and Haiti can all understand each other without much difficulty, even though each patois differs from the others. Trinidad and Grenada also had many patois speakers at the beginning of this century, but the old speakers have died out and not many of the present generation can speak patois. When St Lucia and Dominica were eventually taken over by the British, patois was already well established and has remained the language of the people in spite of English becoming the official language and strenuous efforts by teachers and others until recently to eradicate it. Patois affects the way people speak and write English.

Here are some examples:

They were froing stones at the dog. (froing = throwing)

They went in the middle of the pitch. (in = to)

He watched me closely behind a tree. (from behind)

The lady refused to sell for me. (for = to)

Come out in the rain. (Come out of the rain.)

Exercise

Following are sentences produced by children who speak both patois and English. Some of the spellings and phrases in the sentences are peculiar to these children and some are widespread throughout all the West Indies. Convert the sentences into acceptable Standard English.

1   He made my heart reach in my toes.

2   I tolded my friend that I am going and sell some bananas Roseau.

3   My friend and I went by Mr Jumbory.

4   A car was passing and my sister was not mineing her business and a car knock her on the leg. When my mother saw her leg got hurt she bring her to the hospital right away. When my mother reach in the hospital there was only one doctor. So the doctor ask my mother what is wrong with the girl. The doctor was very suprise when she heard what happen and she told my mother that she will keep the child in the hospital.

5   After we had finished playing, I went at my home to eat.

6   After I eat, I whent a sleep.

7   But my sadness all past away when I ran into the kitchen to see what my mother had brought home.

8   When I was baving, I see a snake.

9   As the day come near people prepare them self for Christmas. The day past by so fast it was then Christmas Day.

10   They asked me how many I selling the bananas.

11   On my Christmas holiday I travelled to some of the places I have never went before. Everywhere I pass some people were laughing while others wish their children merry christmas.

12   Almost every body enjoy themself by drinking rum.

13   I help killing the animals.

14   When we saw that they have not arrived, we paid a dollar to make a phone call at Mr Jack.

15   My mother was wateing for me to go to the shop with my brother but the shop was close.

16   The dog came running into our direction.

17   The driver would not take heed to the dangers and the bus landed into a river.

Colloquial language

'Colloquial' is a term used to refer to the kind of language used in conversations, especially among people who are familiar with each other. It is usually casual in tone and the speaker does not pay as much attention to speech as if it were a formal occasion. However, colloquial does not mean non-standard or ungrammatical. Colloquial language differs from formal language in the words used (everyday words rather than learned words); the length of sentences (shorter, simpler sentences); the shortening of words (haven't, can't, he's); the use of elliptical as opposed to full sentences (not saying the whole sentence or leaving out parts because the person listening understands).

Read this passage, which is a discussion between a daughter and mother, written for the most part in Standard English.

'So when did you get the money?'

'So when did you get the money?'

'I didn't get the money, I mean your money. A lawyer sent to call me, said it was about Mrs Blewchamp's will.'

'Did you go?'

'Yes. I was really nervous, but to cut a long story short, he told me she left each one of you fifteen-hundred dollars, me twenty-five hundred dollars, and you her papers and books.'

'Jeez, I wish I knew her. So why can't I get the money?'

'Because that's what the will say – the papers and books you get when you're sixteen or seventeen. There, I'm all done. You said you wanted to talk about Zulma.' I nodded.

'Mum, why can't I have some of the baby bonus money for Zulma to buy her a ticket to go back home – to Tobago?'

'Zulma to buy her a ticket to go back home – to Tobago?'

'Zulma's home is here now Margaret …'

'But Mum she's real unhappy, and just like Mrs Blewchamp was kind to us, can't we be kind to Zulma? Please Mum, it's not a lot – four-hundred and fifty-five dollars.'

'How d'you know that?'

'I called the airlines and asked. Look Mum her stepfather hates her, her mother's kind of scared of him, and Zulma wants to be home with her gran – please.'

'I don't believe in getting involved with other people's business.'

'Other people's business? She's my friend – she's like my sister. No, she's more than my sister, she's not "other people", and it's *my* money – you said it was and I want it.'

'You better watch your mouth child …'

'But *I* need that money, to help my friend. How come I don't have any rights over what is *my* money?'

'Because *I* am your mother and *I* decide *when* and *how* you get it, and that's that.'

'But that's not fair!' I was crying now. 'It's not fair – you go spending all kinds of stupid money on clothes for Jo-Ann and make-up and all kinds of junk we don't need, and you won't give me any of my own money to help my friend. I hate you, I hate this family!'

In the passage the author tries to make the conversation seem normal by using colloquial language. For example:

- There are many shortened words, e.g. didn't, can't, don't, won't, I'm, she's, it's, d'you, that's, you're, gran.

- There are expressions which appear in conversation, e.g. to cut a long story short', 'her mother's kind of scared of him', 'Jeez', 'There. I'm all done', '– please'.

- There is a type of omission that would occur in conversation in the following 'A lawyer sent to call me, said it was about ... '.

- In the punctuation of the passage the dash is used several times to make the sentence run on and to introduce additional and explanatory information, as would happen in a conversation.

The passage on the next page, although it is not a conversation, is partly colloquial because it uses current, familiar expressions, which appeal to the most casual reader. At the same time, however, it uses some very formal English expressions which the casual reader might not understand. In the passage the author is contrasting the modern 'Informal Commercial Importer' with the traditional 'higgler' (called 'huckster' in some parts of the West Indies). The author is mischieviously using a formal title, big words and references to historical figures to give a picture of one version of the higgler today. In other words, just as today's higgler has become fanciful, the language used to describe her is fanciful.

Questions

1   What is the tone of the passage – serious, comic, jokey? Give reasons for your answer.

2   Look up *Boadicea* and *Amazons* in an encyclopedia and then say what the connection is between them and the 'Informal Commercial Importer'.

3   What does 'out-Thatcher, out-Gandhi, out-Meir, Maggie, Indira and Golda' mean? Who are/were these three persons and why are they specifically mentioned in this passage?

THE INFORMAL COMMERCIAL IMPORTER (THE HIGGLER)

Yesterday's Higgler

The un-named male of yesteryear who suggested that females are the weaker sex was obviously a humorist far ahead of his time. Consider if you will what he would have made of Boadicea's 20th Century heiresses, of the latter day Amazons. Consider this little nation where multiple thousands of women could, on their slowest days, out-

the latest manifestation of a long line of dominant women in Jamaica's history, descendants of Nanny, the fabled heroine of Jamaica's colonial days who could, with a twitch of her butt, deflect the bullets of hapless English soldiers, who could floor a man with her fingers, who could . . . well we could go on and on.

Today, there is not one

Thatcher, out-Gandhi, out-Meir, Maggie Indira and Golda without working up a sweat.

Consider Jamaica's Informal Commercial Importers: but

Nanny. There are thousands. Like their matriarch, they too leave "strong" men crying in their wake, they too will never yield to domination by "so-so" man.

In basic terms, I.C.I.'s are traders. They buy and sell. They buy in Miami, Panama City, Port-Au-Prince, and a few other cities, and they sell their stock at flea markets, bend-down-plazas and in other assorted outlets throughout the island. Since the trade began to proliferate in the late seventies/early eighties, I.C.I.'s have moved up-market; no longer taking up yams to sell to finance six-for-99-cent drawers. Now, they're stocking "Miami Vice" wear,

designer dresses, and are selecting which customers they'll supply using criteria as snob-consciously as any limp-wristed hairdresser. I.C.I.'s are rapidly becoming a new elite class, high-cost specialist suppliers who, awash in money, now own much of uptown Kingston through astute and cash-only investments.

SOME CHARACTERSTICS OF JAMAICAN HIGGLERS

Should you wish to enter the ranks of Jamaican higglers, the following are assets:

- Being female. Most higglers are women, and it is felt that certain talents associated with women, e.g. common sense, delight in bargaining, etc., are useful advantages.

- Being unmistakably female. Higglering is a robust occupation. The amply endowed frontally and in the rear are far likelier to endure (and triumph) in the pushing and shoving that takes place.

- Being of a forthcoming disposition. Higglering is not for the faint of heart or for the shrinking violet. In the course of a single day, a higgler may be required to stand up to stewardesses, customs officers, policemen, hotel employees, etc. etc., all of

whom are conspiring to drive her out of business. Any higgler who allows herself to be intimidated might as well pack it in. Air Jamaica stewardesses, at long last, have met their match.

- Being physically fit: Higglering at the I.C.I. level is a consuming occupation. A typical schedule may call for catching the 3:00 a.m./ 11:00 p.m. nightbird flight to Miami on a Thursday night, checking into a Miami dive (4 to a room, napping by rotation), hitting the streets from 7:00 a.m. till 11:00 p.m. on Friday and Saturday and heading home on Sunday.

- Being bilingual. Many higglers acquire bilingual skills which are useful in dealing with customs and immigration officials in other countries. Their importance lies in being able to understand what the official wants while communicating absolute ignorance if such is advisable. Many of these officials are in fact absolutely certain that Jamaicans speak no English. Indeed, after being subjected to a few choice forty-shilling words, they do have a point.

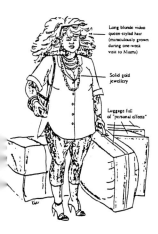

Today's I.C.I.

4   Why does the author use the abbreviation ICI and what effect does he want to create when he says 'Higglering at the ICI level'?

5   Explain examples of colloquial conversation.

6   What does the author mean when he says 'Many higglers acquire bilingual skills'?

7   Describe Yesterday's Higgler and Today's ICI.

8   Write the words from a scene between an ICI and a Customs official.

Assignment   Explain in detail how the speech of a higgler/huckster (in your country) differs from the standard language.

Slang

Slang is the term used to refer to words and phrases used in a novel way. It may be used for perfectly normal English words but with a strikingly new meaning or it may be used for words made up to convey a perfectly normal and familiar meaning. Slang is particularly popular among young people.

   Because the whole point of slang is its novelty, it does not last very long – after a time it either disappears or becomes a normal part of the language. A slang expression has the following life history:

- First stage: an individual (e.g. a disc jockey) uses an expression.

- Second stage: the expression becomes popular with a certain group and is used and over-used.

- The expression is gradually used less frequently and becomes a normal word used by everybody, or it goes out of active use and is forgotten.

The most important characteristic to look for in determining whether expressions are slang is the motive or intention of the speaker/writer. If the speaker wants to give the impression that s/he is up with the latest trends or is a trendsetter, or if s/he is using the language of an in-group or the 'jet-set' type, or if s/he makes it seem as if his/her language is the normal language of artists, actors, athletes, entertainers, singers, then the language will have a slangy tone and contain many slang expressions. Critics and connoisseurs, in order to establish their credentials, usually use slang expressions.

Exercise

Read the following passage, picking out all the expressions you would regard as slang

> In 1980 Lighthouse and his brothers got together and started a band styled Hard Rockers. After three months they brought in a special drummer, Brother D, and they began billing themselves as Hard Rockers + D. They released three singles in quick succession which turned into smash hits. Lighthouse himself could not read music but his youngest brother, Deeza, had aced the course at the School of Music, and it was he who put out some hard notes on paper for the rest of the band.
>
> Lighthouse's lyrics were tough and uncompromising, so much so that the Mango label turned gold again and again. No pop single had ever shot up the charts as fast as the monumental 'O Sadamite', which was backed up on the flip side by Brother D's drum version. The title track on the band's first album was another scorcher. 'Italiation' was voted 'tune of the year' and it made the album 'album of the year' in 1984. The next album bombed, however. It was way out and the fans just could not reach it, so Deeza had to bring down some of the tunes a notch while Brother D simplified the beat. When this album was reissued later the fans lapped it up.
>
> On their first tour Hard Rockers + D faced a hostile press in some cities, but by the time the tour had ended, the hard, haunting tones of Lighthouse and the powerful rhythms of Brother D had them jigging and bopping and standing in awe.

Assignment

Imagine you were telling a group of unsophisticated elderly people who understand Standard English reasonably well and who live in a rural village in your country about Lighthouse and the band and you had to get over in everyday Standard English the information in the passage above. How would you do it? In other words, rewrite the passage, remove the slang expressions and give it a conservative tone.

Section B Language work

Vocabulary

Exercise

Underline the words in the following which in normal speech are stressed for emphasis:

X: You don't seem to me as if you are interested in school.
Y: I am interested.

X: Did you do your homework or did someone do it for you?
Y: I did it.

X: You did not do your homework the day before, did you?
Y: I did do it.
X: Tell me who really did it.
Y: You don't believe me even when I am telling the truth.

X: I don't believe you because you are not.
Y: How can you say that?

X: It must be true. It shows in your eyes.
Y: I am not telling lies and nothing is showing in my eyes.

X: You were a liar. You are a liar. You will always be a liar.
Y: That's what you think. I know better.

X: You will end up in jail. Believe me.
Y: I don't care what you say.

X: I am well aware of that. Who or what do you care about?
Y: That's my business.

X: Please leave this room at once.
Y: Thank you.

Punctuation

Exercise

Restore the punctuation and capital letters in the following passages.

1   yes please enrol me as a member and send me my four triple volumes shown here containing twelve mysteries i enclose no money now i may examine my books for ten days then will either accept all four volumes for only $1 plus shipping or return them and owe nothing

2   the arrival of peregrine roderick clyde browne on earth was authenticated by his birth certificate his father was named as oscar motley clyde browne occupation solicitor and his mother as marguerite diana clyde browne maiden name churley their address was the cones pinetree lane virginia water it was also announced in the times with the additional note most grateful thanks to the staff of st barnabas nursing home

3   no matter who says it it's an amazing deal any three books for just $3 plus shipping and handling and you don't have to buy any more books ever no bull but why not browse through these pages and see for yourself if you're a history buff there's battle cry of freedom james mcpherson's history of the civil war or for a different type of history try stephen hawking's a brief history of time for lovers of fiction we've got toni morrison's haunting novel beloved which won the 1988 pulitzer prize and the accidental tourist now an award winning film

Spelling

Common spelling errors

The major problem with spelling is that you often do not realise when your spelling is wrong. In other words, your own spelling often does not seem abnormal or doubtful to you. Look at the following examples of spelling which seemed quite right to those who wrote them:

Wrong spelling	*Right spelling*
on till	until
sosage	sausage
breadfast	breakfast
concensus	consensus (consent)
intrest	interest
wrost meat	roast meat
voilence	violence
the order children	the other children
chior practice	choir practice
whent	went
uneform	uniform
bage [a colour]	beige
Febuary	February
thought in steps	taught in steps

There is no simple and quick way to overcome this kind of wrong spelling and to become familiar with the correct spelling. Familiarity usually comes with practice and practice means reading and writing more.

Homophones

In addition to the mistakes mentioned above, mistakes are made with many common words in English which sound alike but differ in meaning. In the case of such words, called 'homophones', it is helpful to study them and to keep near at hand a list of them so that when you have to use any of them, you can refer to the list in order to be sure that your spelling corresponds with the meaning that you intend.

air: the atmosphere
ere: before
e'er: ever
heir: an inheritor

altar: place for worship
alter: to change

ball: a round body
bawl: to shout

bare: uncovered
bear: an animal, to endure

beer: a drink
bier: coffin, tomb, grave

being: present participle of 'be'
been: past participle of 'be'

berry: a small fruit
bury: to put into the ground

berth: place for ship
birth: coming into life

boar: a male pig
bore: to pierce

brake: to reduce speed
break: to shatter

boughs: parts of a tree
bows: bends at the waist

coarse: rough, not fine
course: a series of lessons

cord: string
chord: combination of notes

core: the heart
corps: a body of men

council: an assembly
counsel: to advise

currant: small dried grape
current: stream

desert: dry arid land
dessert: sweet dish

doe: a female deer
dough: paste for baking

dying: giving up life
dyeing: changing the colour

faint: weak
feint: a pretence

forth: onwards
fourth: next after third

foul: not clean
fowl: a bird

fur: covering of animals
fir: a tree

gait: manner of walking
gate: a door

holy: pure, sacred
wholly: altogether

in: into
inn: a tavern

isle: an island
aisle: passage between pews

key: part for a lock
quay: a wharf

knead: to work dough
need: to require

lain: reclined
lane: an alley

led: past form of 'lead'
lead: a metal

lessen: make less
lesson: instruction

marshal: arrange
martial: military

meat: flesh
meet: to encounter
mete: to measure

medal: designed piece of metal
meddle: to interfere

might: power
mite: an insect

miner: one who mines
minor: person under 21; lesser

oar: for a boat
ore: metal
o'er: over

pain: suffering
pane: piece of glass

pair: a couple
pare: to cut
pear: a fruit

peak: top, pointed end
pique: ill-will

peer: an equal, to look
pier: wharf

peal: a loud sound
peel: to remove skin

plain: level ground
plane: a tool, aeroplane

pole: a piece of wood
poll: voters, voting

pore: an opening
pour: to empty out

practice: a custom (noun)
practise: to do repeatedly (verb)

praise: commend
prays: entreats
preys: plunders

principal: chief
principle: rule

profit: gain
prophet: one who foretells

reign: rule
rein: controls for an animal

raise: to lift up
rays: lines of light
raze: to demolish

rap: to knock
wrap: to surround with

read: interpret writing
reed: a plant

right: not wrong
rite: a ceremony
write: form letters
wright: a craftsman

ring: a circle, sound a bell
wring: to twist

root: part of a plant
route: path to follow

rote: memory
wrote: past of 'write'

row: a line, to move a boat with
    oars
roe:eggs of a fish

rye: type of grain
wry: crooked

sear: to burn
seer: a prophet

sew: to join with stitches
sow: to plant seeds
so: thus

cite: quote
site: place
sight: vision

soar: to mount
sore: painful

soul: spirit
sole: part of the foot

stake: a post, money bet
steak: a slice of beef

stationary: fixed
stationery: paper for writing

straight: not crooked
strait: narrow

team: a side, a group
teem: to be full of

tear: from the eye
tier: a row

they're: they are
their: of them
there: in that place

threw: part of 'throw'
through: from end to end

time: season
thyme: plant

trait: feature
tray: for carrying

vain: conceited
vein: a blood-vessel
vane: a weather-cock

vale: valley
veil: used for covering the face

ware: goods
wear: to have on the body

yoke: a chain
yolk: yellow of an egg

Exercise

Use each of the following pairs in a single sentence to make clear the difference in meaning and use between the two words:

1 Britain   Briton
2 canon   cannon
3 cellar   seller
4 cymbal   symbol
5 cite   site
6 descent   dissent
7 metal   mettle
8 weather   whether
9 compliment   complement
10 council   counsel
11 martial   marshal
12 principal   principle
13 stationary   stationery
14 sweet   suite
15 statue   stature

Acknowledgements

The author and publishers are grateful to the following for permission to reproduce copyright material:

Aitken, Stone & Wylie Limited for an extract from *Miguel Street* by V.S. Naipaul

Anvil Press Poetry Ltd. for the poem, 'Don't talk to me About Bread' by E.A. Markham from *E.A. Markham: Human Rites, 1984*

Dr. Bridget Brereton and *The Journal of Caribbean History* for an extract from the article on John Jacob Thomas

Caribbean Examinations Council for an extract of 1991 statistics from *Appendix I of Report on the work of candidates for 1. English A 2. English B*

The Centre for Management, Bridgetown, for the poem, 'Ole times' by Paul Douglas from *The Shape of things to Come* , eds. Paul King & Stanley Reid, 1972

Caribbean Development Bank, St. Michael, for Appendix 2 of 'Agricultural Diversification in the Caribbean Community: Some Issues' (Statement by the then President, Mr. William G. Demas, at the Seventeenth annual Meeting of the board of Governors) 1987

Mrs. Flora Coard for the extract, 'Man struck with a gru-gru stick' from *Bitter Sweet & Spice: These Things I remember* by F.M. Coard

The Copyright Organisation of Trinidad & Tobago Ltd. for the song 'Solomon Out' composed by Slinger Francisco/The Mighty Sparrow/COTT; the poem: 'Haiti' by David Rudder

CPS Caribbean Communications, Inc for the map of Charlestown from *The St. Kitts-Nevis Traveller Tourist Guide* Vol. 3 no 1. April, 1990

The Archives of Claude McKay, Carl Cowl, Administrator for the poem 'If We Must Die' by Claude McKay published in *Selected Poems of Claude McKay* by Harcourt Brace Jovanovich

Andre Deutsch Ltd. for an extract from *Green Days by the River* by Michael Anthony. 1967, 1973

DHL Worldwide Express for their advertisement

Editors Press Service, Inc. for 'Where Will New Woman Find a Man' by William Raspberry

Faber and Faber Ltd. for 'A Far Cry from Africa' from *Collected Poems* by Derek Walcott

Fernandes Distillers (1973) Limited for the advert, 'Fernandes Vat 19 Rum' © and reproduction rights are reserved

John Gilmore for an extract from the article *The St. Paul's Gazebo*

The Gleaner Company Ltd., for 'Gleaner Advertising' and the article 'The Graduates look good, but are they?' from *The Sunday Gleaner*, 9 July, 1989

Victor Gollancz for the letter, 'One illustration' from *Rosa* by Rosa Guy

Hamish Hamilton Ltd. for an extract from *The State of the Language* by P. Howard

Heinemann Publishers (Oxford) Ltd., for an extract from *Harrier's Daughter* by M Noursbe Philip. Heinemann Educational

David Higham Associates, for an extract from *Let Sleeping Vets Lie* by James Herriot; the poem, *Ballad of the Landlord* by Langston Hughes. Publ. Vintage.

The Independent Newspaper Publishing plc, for the article 'A controversial oral exam in English' by Nicholas Bagnall, reproduced in *The Independent*, 30 July 1987

Jamrite Cultural Dissemination Committee, Jamrite Publications, Kingston, for an extract from the *How to be a Jamaican Handbook*, 1988

Longman Group UK, for 'Tears of the Sea' from *Arrival of the Snake Woman and Other Stories* by Olive Senior

Martin Secker & Warburg Ltd. for an extract from *Vintage Stuff* by Tom Sharpe

Estate of Edgar Mittelholzer and The Bodley Head for and extract from *My Bones and my Flute* by Edgar Mittelholzer

Mutabaruka for the poem *Free Up De Lan*

'Till I collect' from *Poems of Succession* by Martin Carter, published by New Beacon Books, 1977

Velma Newton for an extract from The *Silver Men: West Indian Labour Migration to Panama 1850-1914*. Kingston, Jamaica: I.S.E.R., U.W.I, 1984; reprinted 1987

Oxford University Press for the poem 'Horse Weebles' by Edward Kamau Brathwaite from *Mother Poem* © Edward Kamau Brathwaite, 1977

Penguin Books Ltd. for an extract from *Old Goriot* by Balzac translated by Marion Ayton

Reckitt and Colman Products Limited for Disprin pack instructions

Crawford (Penguin classics, 1951), copyright © Marion Ayton Crawford, 1951

Sangster's Book Stores Ltd., for the poem 'Bans O' Killing' from *Jamaica Labrish* by Louise Bennett

Mrs. Ruby St. John wife of Bruce St. John and Mrs. Joy St John-Carrington daughter of Bruce St. John for the poem 'West coast sea' by Bruce St. John

Sterling Health for *Panadol* pack instructions

Yale University Press for an extract from *After Africa* by R. Abrahams and J. Szwed, 1983

Zimbabwe Publishing House (Pvt.) Ltd. for an extract from *Coming of the Dry Season* by Charles Mungoshi

The publishers are grateful to the following for permission to reproduce photographs:

Anne Bolt, pages 25, 49, 84, 111; Stephanie Colasanti, page 119; Tony Hardwell, page 150; David Simson, page 151; Mark Edwards/Still Pictures, pages 57, 100; Mary Evans Picture Library, pages 59, 103; Robert Harding Picture Library, page 86; London Features International, page 75; Panos pictures page 109; Redferns, page 95; Bob Thomas Sports Photography, page 41.

Cover photo: Tony Stone Worldwide

Index